DISCIPLINES AS FRAMEWORKS
FOR STUDENT LEARNING

DISCIPLINES AS

FRAMEWORKS FOR

STUDENT LEARNING

Teaching the Practice
of the Disciplines

Edited by

Tim Riordan and James Roth

STERLING, VIRGINIA

COPYRIGHT © 2005 BY
STYLUS PUBLISHING, LLC

Published by Stylus Publishing, LLC
22883 Quicksilver Drive
Sterling, Virginia 20166-2102

Library of Congress Cataloging-in-Publication Data
Disciplines as frameworks for student learning :
teaching the practice of the disciplines / edited by Tim
Riordan and James Roth.—1st ed.
 p.   cm.
 Includes index.
 ISBN 1-57922-122-X (cloth : alk. paper)—
 ISBN 1-57922-123-8 (pbk. : alk. paper)
  1. College teaching—United States.
 2. Interdisciplinary approach in education—United
States.   3. Universities and colleges—Curricula—
United States.   I. Riordan, Tim, 1948–   II. Roth,
James Leonard, 1945–
LB2331.D544   2004
378.1′25—dc22   2004006317

ISBN: 1-57922-122-X (cloth)
ISBN: 1-57922-123-8 (paper)

Printed in the United States of America

All first editions printed on acid-free paper
that meets the American National Standards Institute
Z39-48 Standard.

First Edition, 2005

10 9 8 7 6 5 4 3 2 1

CONTENTS

PREFACE

In her 2004 essay in the *Carnegie Foundation Perspective* series, Pat Hutchings makes the point that "Teaching, like any craft or art, advances when people find like-minded colleagues to work with, to review their efforts, and push them to the next stages of thinking." There could not be a better description of the process that led to the writing of this book, nor, indeed, of what the book is intended to be. The authors of this work are colleagues who have collaborated over an extended period of time on what it means to approach disciplines as frameworks for student learning. They have both encouraged and challenged one another to articulate their practice as teachers and the principles that ground that practice. And they have certainly pushed one another to stages of thinking beyond what they might have imagined.

How often do chemistry and English professors explore together the similar kinds of thinking they want students to learn in their respective disciplines? What teaching issues bring a mathematician and historian together to consider ways of engaging their students in the practice of their disciplines? Why might a professor of economics find some of the same tensions in teaching her discipline as a professor of philosophy? Is it possible that faculty from such a wide array of disciplines could identify the unique characters of their disciplines and still agree on some fundamental principles for the design of teaching, learning, and assessment?

These questions suggest the intellectual and pedagogical issues at the heart of the collaboration that shaped this book. The phrase, "disciplines as frameworks for student learning," first emerged in discussions of a cross-disciplinary group of Alverno College faculty who met regularly to explore pedagogical strategies and issues within and across disciplines. It had become clear that there was pedagogical power in using teaching and learning as the lens for inquiry into one's discipline. In the course of those discussions it was suggested that a few faculty from different disciplines write reflections on what it meant for them to think of their disciplines as frameworks for student learning. After writing initial drafts, they shared those reflections with their colleagues at Alverno College and then at the 2002 annual American Association for Higher Education (AAHE) conference in Chicago.

Hutchings also makes the point in her essay that we need "structures and habits for exchange across the emergent communities of conversation about teaching and learning," and that the resulting exchange "would lead to a healthy cross-fertilization of practices and to a greater awareness of common underlying principles." The authors of this book have been part of an institutional culture that fosters this kind of exchange among the faculty, and this is reflected in the frequent reference of the authors to the work of their colleagues. In this spirit, it is important to acknowledge at the outset that the authors represent a faculty that takes collective responsibility for making disciplines frameworks for student learning. The book is an effort to extend our discourse on teaching and learning to our colleagues across the higher education community, and we hope that the idea of disciplines as frameworks for student learning is particularly helpful in promoting and enriching that discourse.

THE AUTHORS

Lucy Cromwell is professor of English at Alverno College. She holds a Ph.D. in English from the University of Wisconsin, Milwaukee.

Zohreh Emami is professor of economics and associate dean for academic affairs at Alverno College. She holds a Ph.D. in economics from Michigan State University.

Donna Engelmann is professor of philosophy at Alverno College. She holds a Ph.D. in philosophy from Marquette University.

Ann van Heerden is associate professor of chemistry at Alverno College. She holds a Ph.D. in biochemistry from the University of Texas at Austin.

Susan Pustejovsky is associate professor of mathematics at Alverno College. She holds a Ph.D. in mathematics from Marquette University.

Tim Riordan is professor of philosophy and associate dean for academic affairs at Alverno College. He holds a Ph.D. in philosophy of education from Marquette University.

James Roth is professor of history at Alverno College. He holds a Ph.D. in history from the University of California, Berkeley.

Rebecca Valentine is an alumna of Alverno College in English and philosophy. She is a professional writer in Windsor, Colorado.

INTRODUCTION

Tim Riordan

During my first year of graduate school studying philosophy I took a course on Aristotle, and as part of our final examination, my teacher required that each student meet with him to discuss two significant concepts from Aristotle's metaphysics. I selected Aristotle's notions of "nature" and "substance" as the focus for the exam. These were obvious and relatively safe choices, and I felt well versed in them when I walked into the professor's office. I was not prepared for what he then said to me: "Explain to me as you would to your grandparents what Aristotle means by nature and substance and why anyone should care about those ideas." I was in shock, but gathered myself and joked, "Well, both my grandparents have doctorates in philosophy, so . . ." He appreciated my recovery but insisted I proceed.

To be honest, I don't remember much of what I said after that, but I have always remembered the moment and consider it one of the best learning experiences I had in my entire graduate education. It was perhaps the only time that a graduate school professor asked me to think explicitly about how I would actually teach what I was learning about philosophy. He also knew that how well I could teach the ideas I was studying would be some measure of how well I had learned them. In my nearly thirty years of teaching, I have often thought of that incident, and each time I learn a little more from it in light of my own experiences.

In my initial reflection on this graduate school experience, I was especially struck by the fact that my teacher was asking me to think about philosophy as a framework for learning for my future students. He was, in effect, letting me know that my success as a teacher would depend not merely on how well I understood an idea but also on how well I could help others care about it, understand it, and use it. In fact, it challenged me to ask myself just what it was I hoped students would learn by studying philosophy. The fact that my professor had asked me to teach my grandparents also reminded me that many of the students I would be teaching in the future would not necessarily have an initial interest in philosophy and would not aspire to do extended study in the discipline. I concluded that what really mattered was not so much whether they remembered what Aristotle said but whether they had developed habits of mind that would serve them well.

This has made a big difference in the way I now think about what it means to be a scholarly teacher. My primary role as an educator is to create ways of assisting students to make philosophy a framework of learning for themselves, so my scholarship extends beyond study of philosophy to reflection on how I can help students use it. I should add here that this kind of reflection is as intellectually challenging and rewarding as what we have traditionally thought of as scholarly research. Creating ways to make a discipline come alive for those who are not experts requires rigorous thought about what really matters in a field and how to engage students in its practice. As the authors in this book demonstrate, approaching a discipline as a framework for learning means that they ask questions of their fields that might otherwise be ignored.

In this book, faculty from a variety of liberal arts disciplines reflect on what it has meant for them to approach their disciplines as frameworks for student learning. They provide what might be considered intellectual autobiographies with a focus on how their thinking and practice have been affected by their identity as educators in their respective disciplines. The authors make it clear that serious reflection on disciplines as frameworks for student learning requires more than developing a set of techniques in the classroom. Although each writes out of his or her own disciplinary expertise, all of them address similar questions in one way or another, questions they see as essential in making their disciplines truly become frameworks for student learning:

- What should students be able to do and how should they be able to think as a result of study in a discipline?
- What does learning in the disciplines look like at different developmental levels?
- How do faculty design learning and assessment in the disciplines?

- How do faculty approach study of their disciplines with student learning as their primary focus?
- What institutional structures and processes can assist faculty to engage and teach their disciplines as frameworks for student learning?

Student Learning Focus

When my philosophy professor asked me to think about how I would teach Aristotle's ideas to my grandparents, he was reminding me that my primary professional role would be to teach students to understand and think in my discipline. A consistent theme throughout the book is the transforming effect on faculty when they make student learning the center for deliberation on their disciplines. There is much talk in higher education today about being "student centered," but the authors in this book are more specific in the way they think about this. They emphasize the value and implications of being "student-learning centered." For example, all of the authors stress the need to articulate clear learning outcomes for their students, and they focus on learning outcomes that describe how students think in and use the disciplines they study. For example, in the chapter on chemistry Ann van Heerden describes not only how she would characterize thinking in chemistry, but also how she wants students to practice and demonstrate such thinking and how that informs her teaching.

This emphasis on ways of thinking in and using the disciplines includes a deep concern for mastery of the concepts and perspectives at the heart of a field of study. In fact, the authors explain that in many instances students demonstrate their knowledge and understanding most effectively when they are able to apply what they have studied to personal, professional, and civic contexts. Whether in design of learning experiences or of assessment processes, the authors consistently report that they continually require their students to practice the disciplines. They have come to see, as much research on learning has shown, that mastery of a subject is more likely to occur when people actively engage in the practice of what they are studying. In other words, mastery of content or subject is demonstrated and enhanced by active use. It is not a matter of mastering the content and then using it.

The authors of the following chapters also take seriously reflection on who their students are and how they learn, because they recognize that their success as teachers depends not only on what they know about their respective fields but also on what they know about their students. As a result, they understand the need to be familiar with the literature on learning theories and learning styles as well as some of the most recent research in cognitive science. Just as important, they know, is creating ways of identifying the learning needs of the particular students they are teaching at any given time. Designing assignments and classroom experiences that allow the teacher to get a sense of student learning needs is critical in coming to understand the most effective ways to engage students in the practice of disciplines. Disciplines serve as frameworks for student learning more effectively when the students are in the frame.

Learning as Developmental

Another critical dimension of the insights offered in the book is the careful attention to learning as a developmental process. What are the differences, for example, between the kind of thinking we might expect of students who are just beginning study of a field and those who are ready to graduate? How do we design courses in our disciplines that consciously assist students to develop as learners rather than simply move from the study of one thing to another? The authors take up these and other related questions and give examples of how they have come to think about and design learning developmentally in their disciplines.

In the chapters on history and mathematics, James Roth and Susan Pustejovsky focus primarily on teaching students who are not history or math majors. Roth makes the point that too often students who take only one or two courses in history spend much of their time "absorbing the conclusions of historians" without ever having the experience of actually engaging in the methods of the discipline and considering their benefits and limitations. He then goes on to explore how he designs learning for students who are often novices in the field, whether they are majors or not, in order to foster historical thinking appropriate to the level of the students.

Designing Learning and Assessment

When my Aristotle professor asked me to explain philosophical concepts to my grandparents, he challenged me to think about ways that would actually assist the learner to understand and use those concepts. He was also assessing my understanding of Aristotle by having me try to teach his ideas to someone else. In other words, my professor's assessment, or exam, was based on the idea that I could best demonstrate my own understanding of the concepts by my ability to use them, in this case teach them. I also recall that during the course of my response the professor would occasionally stop me with a question or comment, pointing out that I wasn't being as clear as I could be or wondering out loud how my grandparents would respond to what I had just said. He was giving me feedback that helped me think about how I might improve my performance.

The authors in this book explore how the learning they have identified as significant for their students in their respective disciplines has affected the way they design learning experiences and assessments. The principles my professor either consciously or unconsciously applied are reflected in the analyses provided by the authors here. They consciously shape their teaching around the ways of thinking they want their students to develop within and across their disciplines; they design assessments that require students to demonstrate their thinking and understanding through application and use; they provide continuous feedback to help students improve. In writing about English as a framework for student learning, for example, Lucy Cromwell explicitly identifies the learning outcomes her department has articulated for their majors and then describes how the assignments and assessment she creates are consciously built on the cognitive processes embodied in those outcomes.

One other principle that the authors emphasize in their respective chapters is the importance and impact of student self assessment. After all, students must eventually be able to assess their own performance, not merely rely on their instructors to assess them. You will note that throughout the book, the authors spell *self assessment* without a hyphen. They do this intentionally because they wish to emphasize the point they make with their students, that the student is the agent, not the object, of her assessment. She is not literally assessing herself but assessing her performance in a specific context.

Scholarly Inquiry into One's Discipline

Implied in my philosophy professor's approach to assessing my understanding was his conviction that studying Aristotle was no guarantee that I would be able to teach his ideas effectively. The national debate about the relationship between research and teaching tends to revolve around the extent to which doing serious research necessarily enhances the quality of teaching. The authors in this book move beyond that kind of debate to reflection on how their role as educators affects the kind of inquiry they do in their disciplines. What kinds of questions do you ask of a discipline when trying to determine what it has to offer students? What does it mean to be "current" in your discipline when it is your responsibility to assist students of varying interests and needs to learn the discipline? What forms of scholarly inquiry are most effective in approaching disciplines as frameworks for student learning? These are questions that may not be asked often as graduate students prepare for their work as future faculty, or even that present faculty members are accustomed to thinking about very explicitly; however, they are central to the kind of reflection offered in this book.

The authors in this book all address these questions in one form or another, but they come at them from different angles. In the chapters on economics and philosophy, Zohreh Emami and Donna Engelmann raise significant questions about the nature of their disciplines as they have been traditionally practiced, and then consider the implications of their questions for pedagogical practice. The authors in the other chapters are not as concerned with a critique of their disciplines but do challenge assumptions about what it means to teach them. In all of the chapters the authors do articulate their own relationship to their disciplines and how teaching has shaped that relationship.

Creating a Learning Culture

Although the principles and practices articulated in this book should be helpful in any context, the authors all make the point that the particular learning culture of their institution has supported and enhanced their work with disciplines as frameworks for student learning. With this in mind, it might be helpful to describe some dimensions of that culture in order to provide a curricular and institutional backdrop for their remarks and also to suggest ways of creating a context to enhance student learning.

The core curriculum at Alverno College, a liberal arts college for women, has as one of its graduation requirements that all students demonstrate eight abilities characterizing the liberal arts graduate. These abilities have been articulated and constantly refined by the faculty and are taught and assessed in the context of disciplinary and interdisciplinary courses across the curriculum. These abilities are communication, analysis, problem solving, valuing in decision making, social interaction, developing a global perspective, effective citizenship, and aesthetic engagement. Faculty design their courses integrating the teaching of the abilities with their respective disciplinary contexts, and they work with those abilities that they see as central to their fields. For example, while all faculty teach and assess for communication and analysis, an ability such as aesthetic engagement is more likely to be taught in the arts and humanities. The authors of this book give examples of this ability-based learning throughout the chapters.

Although this book is organized by disciplines, it is important to emphasize that the authors are as engaged in cross-disciplinary work as they are in the teaching and study of their own fields. First of all, the faculty at Alverno serve not only in a discipline department but also in one of the ability departments representing each of the eight abilities; this means that they are consistently involved in cross-disciplinary discourse regarding the meaning of the abilities, the ways of teaching and assessing those abilities, and the ways students learn to transfer abilities from one learning context to another. The faculty have also designed several significant interdisciplinary courses in the curriculum (e.g., introductory arts, humanities, and natural science courses) and several interdisciplinary majors (e.g., Communication, Management, and Technology; Community Leadership and Development; Environmental Science; and Global Studies). The authors in this book also indicate that even when teaching their own disciplines they stress the importance of making connections across disciplines and assisting their students to do so. In fact, they suggest that they cannot teach their disciplines effectively without attention to other disciplines. It is clear in Donna Engelmann's chapter on philosophy, for example, that her approach to teaching her discipline is informed by insights from sociology, psychology, and political science. It is interesting that in the chapter written from the student perspective, she comments consistently on the interdisciplinary dimension of her learning as well.

All of the authors comment in one way or another on how collaboration with colleagues within and across disciplines has affected and enhanced their development as scholarly teachers and contributed to the quality of learning for students. There is a rich tradition of this kind of collaboration at Alverno College, where all of the authors have taught or studied. For example, no classes are scheduled at the college on Friday afternoons, so that faculty can work together on issues of teaching, learning, and assessment. In addition, there are three College Institutes during the year, one at the beginning of each semester and one at the end of the academic year, also devoted to collaboration on similar issues. These institutes are similar to three-day conferences, and they are designed by and for the faculty and academic staff at the college. It may be that other institutions do not have that kind of formal collaborative structure in place, but the principle of taking collective responsibility for student learning, and the notion of developing structures that foster the collaboration necessary to act on that principle, are important to consider in any institutional context.

Organization and Focus of Chapters

The chapters in this book focus on specific disciplines as frameworks for student learning, but they are also organized around significant issues that have emerged for the authors in their teaching. We have paired chapters that explore most explicitly and deeply a particular issue, and we think it is significant that these pairings emerged as the authors started to write their own chapters, not as preconceived connections imposed on the structure of the book. In light of this it is interesting to note what some might consider "unlikely" pairings of disciplines that are not always seen as closely related to one another. History and mathematics, for example, may be very different disciplines in some respects, but in this book the authors of those two chapters both consider how to make their disciplines meaningful for students who may initially view them as irrelevant—an issue they both encounter regularly in the teaching of their fields. The chapters on philosophy and economics are paired because both authors find that they are challenged to consider the meanings of their disciplines for those who traditionally have been ignored or viewed as outsiders. And the faculty writing on English and chemistry both emphasize what they have learned about how to teach the cognitive processes of their disciplines to their students. Each of these themes is actually addressed either directly or indirectly in all of the chapters, but the emphasis varies. The book also includes a chapter written by an Alverno graduate, Rebecca Valentine, who reflects on her own experience of learning and how disciplines have functioned and continue to function as frameworks for her learning. We thought it important to include a student voice, and it was gratifying for the other authors to see some of the ideas she emphasized that reflected themes similar to those in the other chapters. This was especially striking since she wrote her chapter before seeing the chapter on English, her college major.

It is important to conclude this introduction by pointing out two very important dimensions that are not explored at length in this book. First, the chapters are organized according to disciplines, and fairly traditional disciplines at that. There is not extended treatment of interdisciplinary or cross-disciplinary frameworks for learning. We decided to focus on specific disciplines because faculty, generally speaking, still tend to identify with a discipline. On the other hand, throughout the book the authors do make reference to the relationships of their disciplines to others, the roles of other disciplines in the teaching of their own, and to the changing scope of their disciplines. Indeed, some of the authors are in one way or another raising questions about whether their disciplines need to be transformed into new disciplines, or at least quite different versions of their own. This is clearly fertile ground for further study that goes beyond the scope of this book.

The reader will also notice that there are no chapters on fields beyond the liberal arts, specifically the professional areas. This, too, can be misleading because it may give the impression that the issues and principles explored here do not relate to teaching in the professions, or that the professions and liberal arts have little connection to one another. This is very far from the case, however. In fact, one of the undercurrents throughout this book is the role of liberal arts disciplines for students who do not major in those fields, and those students are often majors in professional areas such as education, business, and nursing. In discussing the ideas in this book with our colleagues in the professional areas we have already begun to develop analyses of how those areas serve as frameworks for student learning and how the liberal arts and the professions work together in that capacity.

Finally, we see the primary purpose of this book as fostering productive and sustained discourse among our colleagues in higher education, no matter what their disciplines, about the ways we all can engage students in the practice of our disciplines so that disciplines become what the word implies—habits of mind that inform student lives in their various contexts and communities. We have found that kind of discourse vital to our scholarship as educators in our fields and offer the ideas in this book as some measure of the fruits of that work.

PART ONE

LEARNING IN "IRRELEVANT" DISCIPLINES

James Roth (history) and Susan Pustejovsky (mathematics) articulate the challenge of encountering beginning students who have already formed strong (and generally erroneous) perspectives on their disciplines. Whether they think it's a case of memorizing events that have already taken place or going through routine steps to discover answers that are in the back of the book, students tend at first to find these disciplines irrelevant to their lives.

Roth explains the importance of engaging beginning general education history students in the active practice of historical thinking, rather than using such courses primarily to lay the knowledge groundwork for more active learning in later courses. If the popular view of history as a mimetic representation of past reality is not challenged, most of those students will stop studying history as soon as they can. Pustejovsky explores strategies for convincing students of mathematics that they can be active participants in formulating and solving real problems that are important in their academic studies and in their lives.

COMMON GROUND

How History Professors and Undergraduate
Students Learn through History

James Roth

Teaching history as a framework for student learning means moving away
from the practice of presenting semester-long narratives for students to as-
similate and instead engaging them in more active learning, perhaps in creating their own narrative interpretations or raising critical questions about the
underlying motives and assumptions of the historians they read or listen to
in the classroom. This type of learning is often found in advanced undergraduate courses in historiography and in research methods and is the basis
of most graduate-school work. In these active learning situations, history
teachers devote less class time to transmitting a synthesis of the products of
historical scholarship and more to modeling the process by which historians
come to make research-based knowledge claims and to critically appraise the
contributions of other historians to a growing body of historical knowledge.
Instead of lecturing extensively, these teachers work side by side with their
students in a collaborative investigation of historical problems, much as mas-
ters and apprentices in a craft.

Unfortunately, this is a kind of learning that usually touches only a tiny
fraction of the total number of students enrolled in all history courses, from
beginning surveys to graduate seminars. Even the undergraduate history
major, unless she has some independent exposure to the practice of historians, may spend time in four to six lower division history courses absorbing
the conclusions of historians before ever being asked to consider the episte-

mology behind learning in history. These teacher-centered basic courses have been justified in terms of building up a knowledge base that will eventually enable more sophisticated thinking about historical problems. The reality, however, is that most students will stop studying history long before they can benefit from the type of historical thinking for which their professors have been laying the groundwork. A great many students come to their first college history course already prepared to dismiss the subject as irrelevant because they believe it simply retells the story of what has already happened. Passive learning in introductory courses does little to change that popular view of history as a mimetic presentation of past reality. If we really believe that thinking historically or having a historical consciousness provides indispensable insight into the human experience, then we cannot afford to let the potential for affecting most of our students slip through our fingers.

Just as historians sometimes consider whether we can have a greater impact on culture and society by writing for an educated public rather than for other specialists, so too is it possible to consider whether we can have a greater influence as teachers in the area of general education than as preparers of a new generation of scholars. Although I am arguing in this chapter in favor of teaching to the broader range of students, this doesn't have to be an either/or proposition. Insofar as history majors share the same foundation courses with their peers who study history as a part of their general education, they too can benefit from an emphasis on history as a framework for learning from the very beginning of their studies.

The historians at Alverno College know from the experience of teaching in an ability-based curriculum, combined with performance-based assessments of student learning in the classroom, that it is possible to prompt active learning in beginning courses by making the classroom less a performance stage for the teacher and more of a workshop for practicing the craft.[1] Later in the chapter I describe some of these active learning and assessment strategies typical of an ability-based history curriculum. But my colleagues and I have also learned that simply modeling the processes of historical discovery that we want students to be able to perform themselves is not necessarily enough to foster learning through the discipline. If we only show them how we and other historians learn through history—how we identify relevant evidence, evaluate it, and draw conclusions, thereby adding to the body of historical knowledge—we are begging the question embedded in the incomplete phrase, "disciplines as frameworks for learning," that serves as the title of this book. When we complete the phrase by asking *what* is to be learned and *by whom*, it may turn out that many of our students are not interested in learning the same things that we are. Simply to make them a part of our world of discovery may cut them off from the possibility of perceiving the relevance of historically minded thinking in their own lives.

Consider what modern European historians take to be a fundamental, and still contested, question about the consequences of the French Revolution: To what extent did the social conservatism of the revolutionary bourgeoisie retard the development of industrial capitalism in France in the early nineteenth century? To the beginning student of history, this may seem to be an irrelevant question because France is today an industrial nation. What does it matter what the French went through to get there or whether it took more years rather than fewer? Even if we point out that this phenomenon of the absorption of new elites by traditional ones affects vital economic development in many parts of the world today, students will not necessarily see the analogy as important to their learning agenda. If students know that successful performance in a course depends on knowing what the teacher says is important, then they can and will find answers to this question in the historical literature we make available to them. We can even teach them to answer it through an examination of original source documents. But will they transfer these historical thinking skills to issues and situations in their lives outside the history classroom?

Common Ground

If we want to assist all students to learn through history, we need to find the common ground between our scholarly use of history to expand the body of historical knowledge and the kinds of questions that will motivate student learning. In my own teaching I have found this common ground by thinking back to a time in my own personal and intellectual development when history first appealed to me as an orientation to the world and as a way of answering questions I had about society. I got to a point in my studies where I felt I could learn more about people and the world by studying history than I could by studying political science or literature or genetics. I don't recall being as interested in specific research questions about historical events as I was in more general aspects of the historian's stance. By taking a broad view, both in time and space, historians showed a willingness to accept and manage change instead of fighting against it as a threat to order. By comparing structures and practices in different times and places, they saw more possibilities for human society than conventional and present-oriented wisdom allowed. This way of thinking related to my specific need to understand the basis for the social hierarchy and social attitudes in the small town where I had grown up. My interest today in the way difference (such as race, class, gender, age, and sexual orientation) is used to create order, stability, and dominant power in society traces back to those early questions. Since I had found my way to history through broad questions such as these, I thought the same thing might work for my students if I could help them articulate their questions and relate them to the study of history.

Looking to our own undergraduate experiences as standards or benchmarks that we expect our students to reach can be dangerous. The fact that we are teachers and scholars is testimony to the distinctiveness of our commitment and our facility as learners. We were not like most of our classmates in history lectures back then, and we are probably even less like our students today. But I am not talking about expecting my students to achieve skill levels in studying history similar to those I exhibited in my undergraduate papers and examinations. I am talking about connecting historical thinking to our broader reflections on the world around us, and this is something that I believe we can have in common with our students, particularly if we pay more attention to articulating those connections than our own professors did when we were students.

Making students' questions central to our teaching of history implies that students should have input into what is taught and learned in history courses. There are, however, some necessary limits to the democratic classroom. Pedagogical resources have to be prepared and books have to be ordered. There are also limits to the subject matter knowledge of individual teachers. Basic courses also serve multiple audiences, including teacher education students who must be prepared for professional proficiency assessments covering certain standard areas of historical knowledge. But perhaps the greatest limitation on direct student input into course content and course design is that many beginning students have difficulty articulating the kinds of general questions that I have raised. They are not accustomed to theorizing about human behavior. As instructors we have to represent student interests imaginatively by trying to put ourselves in their shoes and by voting their proxy in course design decisions. The following two course examples describe how I try to recapture that common learning ground by combining conventional historical subject matter with thematic issues that I hope are relevant for most of my students.

This design process has been easier because of a decision made by the Alverno history faculty many years ago to offer some of our introductory and intermediate courses as focused case studies (e.g., the French Revolution, the United States in the 1960s or in the Progressive Era, fin-de-siècle Vienna) rather than as broad surveys. These courses serve to fulfill general education requirements in the humanities and as foundation courses for our history majors and minors. Our intention is to teach students how to "read" a specific social and cultural environment, to explore the connections between the various value climates of the time and the ways individuals behave and institutions function, and then to be able to apply that skill of contextual interpretation to learn more effectively in later upper-division surveys. The student who takes only these introductory case study courses as a general education requirement will not develop the broad range of cultural knowledge advocated by "cultural literacy" proponents *as a direct result of undergraduate history course instruction*. But we believe that students who have developed skills in historically minded contextual thinking have a greater capacity to develop such literacy as lifelong learners.

This curricular plan gives us the freedom in those introductory case study courses to choose historical subject matter that "fits" closely with the broader questions students may have. In practice we have tended to choose more contemporary eras for these courses. But even when we teach courses that explore much broader expanses of history, we can still engage students in more active and sustained interpretation of selected problems and issues. There is no rule governing survey courses that mandates metronome-like coverage (one week per decade for U.S. history or one week per century for Western or world civilization). Like a musician using rubato technique to compress or stretch out the basic tempo, we can carve out extra time for focused topics within traditional surveys.

For more than twenty years I have taught one version or another of an introductory course focused on the transition to mass industrial society in the late nineteenth and early twentieth centuries. It varies from the Vienna of Sigmund Freud to the coming of the First World War in Europe to the German experiment with democracy after World War I. Each course enables me to explore with students the problems of societies coping with the uncertainty of change. There are obvious parallels with contemporary society in terms of the destabilizing effects of new technology, the challenge to community standards of radical artistic movements, and the impersonal nature of mass society. But more than anything else I hope that students can resonate with the complex "coming of age" feelings in terms of their own "in-between" status as young adults.

I also teach an intermediate level course on the French Revolution primarily for the purpose of making the point that democracy as a system of government (rather than a theory in political philosophy) originated as recently as the revolutions of the late eighteenth century. My purpose for selecting this subject matter is to help students understand that concepts such as democracy and human rights are not self-evident and transcendent truths that are unchangeable and require no critical response from us today. Instead they were original products of discourse in the eighteenth century and continue to be debated in the current world. History offers powerful opportunities for learning that the unchangeable truths of our lives are almost always subject to change, because it allows students to observe a time before the Revolution when democracy was never used as a descriptor of society and when the idea of equal human rights contradicted the conventional understanding of a hierarchical creation.

The point underlying the design of these two courses is that students should not be asked to study a particular topic in history simply because it interests the instructor or because it is a major milestone in a historical narrative about civilization. If we expect students to take history seriously as a tool or an approach to their understanding of themselves and their lives in society, then we need to select the subject matter with them in mind and make a case for the relevance of history to learning something that is or ought to be important to them.

Open Dialogue

Ultimately, the key to maintaining this common ground is not just to select material that the instructor believes will relate to more general student learning concerns, but also to create an open and ongoing dialogue with students about learning in the course. Students need to know why they should expect a clear rationale for the specific historical content of a course, how their existing intellectual skills can serve them in the course, what aspects of historically minded thinking they need to develop, what it means to think historically as opposed to thinking according to the framework of other disciplines, and so forth. Not only does individual learning increase; learning also tends to be more accessible to every student in the course when I make an ongoing effort to clarify what they are setting out to learn and why. Formally, these expectations are made public in the learning outcomes of the course syllabus. In my course on the French Revolution, for example, one of the stated outcomes is the requirement that students "discern various perspectives through the analysis of human behavior in historical context and to empathize with those viewing life from those perspectives." To me, this ability to understand and fairly evaluate the "otherness" of the past is at the very heart of historical thinking. But it takes more than simply publishing such a requirement to make learning happen. These outcomes serve as focal points for ongoing dialogue.

For example, every time I teach a course that includes first-time college history students, I begin with an introduction that distinguishes, perhaps even somewhat hyperbolically, historical study from study in other disciplines. History students must deliberately set aside their assumptions about what they consider to be normal thought and behavior in order to understand people from the past or from other cultures. I ask them to visualize this as "looking over the shoulder" of someone from the past in order to experience that person's angle of vision. They need to suspend their own beliefs in order to consider the possibility that other people may have good reason for doing something that they themselves would never do or for thinking things that would be unimaginable for them today. In order to forestall possible resistance based on the perception that I may be asking them to abandon their own values in favor of others, I make the very explicit point that I am not asking them to accept uncritically the worldviews of others. They have to compare and judge, but only after achieving an understanding that is not skewed by their own assumptions about what is normal.

Clarifying perspective taking as a required strategy is essential because such a stance clearly goes against the grain of beginning students' preferred learning style. According to the cognitive psychologist Sam Wineburg, who has made detailed studies of novice and professional thinking in history, "History is an unnatural act."[2] My experience of teaching beginning students in a number of contexts—history, integrated humanities, communication seminars—tells me that many prefer identity as a learning strategy. They write about themselves. They engage works of fiction when they can identify with a character. Without an open dialogue about learning in history, there would be the potential for a tremendous clash of wills between what history calls for and what beginning students prefer.

Perspective taking continues as a touchstone for learning throughout these courses. For example, if a student attempts to explain the social hierarchy of old-regime France as grounded in differences of wealth, I say that she has forgotten to look over the shoulder of those people to understand that, for them, birthright rather than money was the traditional basis of status. Focusing on the student's forgetting to apply the principle rather than committing a specific factual error is somehow less damaging to her confidence and tends to produce more effective learning in the future, even when the future questions have nothing to do with the original question of determining status in old-regime Europe.

Another characteristic of historical thinking that I discuss with students at the beginning of these courses is the skepticism that most historians show toward claims of essential human nature or universal human experience. Whenever one is tempted to universalize an attitude or a practice by saying "everyone knows . . ." or "people have always . . . ," historians can trace the history of that idea or practice back to a time when no one seriously considered it to be true. In my experience, the threat that this deconstruction of universals poses to students is more than offset by the sense of empowerment they gain when they become convinced that people have always, sooner or later, been able to effect change in their societies.

My efforts to teach students to adopt specific ways of thinking when they study history are made easier by the common commitment of all Alverno College faculty to student development of analytical ability. Each of us in our own ways teaches students how concepts or frameworks from the disciplines organize thinking.[3] These frameworks might be organizing principles, sets of assumptions, guiding theories, or schools of criticism. In psychology courses at roughly the same curricular level as my beginning history courses, for example, students are learning to use theories to anticipate and predict behavior.[4] This "press" toward purposeful, structured, and context-specific thinking becomes a habitual behavior with students when reinforced consistently across the curriculum. Even students who have not previously studied history will have awareness from other courses that learning in a discipline involves particular modes of investigation and will anticipate the need to learn those modes or frameworks in history.

So far I have said nothing about the basics of sources or the nature of adequate proof in history. I know that these are typical topics in many classroom discussions of what it means to think historically. While I certainly want my students, especially those who will go on to major in history, to understand the differences between primary and secondary sources, the various ways to establish the credibility of witnesses, and the importance of chronology for causal imputation, these "tools" are not the first things that come to mind when I think about history as a framework for learning in beginning and intermediate courses. I am more interested in impressing on students that history is an epistemological approach that recognizes that things change all the time, that human experience is diverse and context specific, and that those differences need to be respected in order to be understood. I want liberally educated adults who have studied some history to be able to represent the perspective of history in their engagement with other people over issues in their personal and community lives. To be able to do that effectively in the future requires that they actively practice historical interpretation in the classroom.

Active Learning

As a result of the open classroom dialogue about assumptions and purposes of historical thinking, my beginning students have an abstract idea of what it means to learn historically. But in order to internalize that set of intellectual skills, they need to practice history themselves. History is a mental process of thinking about human behavior in a particular social context. Students cannot understand the perspective of someone from the past unless they first know some of the material conditions of their lives or the value systems at work in their societies. That is the reason that so many introductory courses in American, Western, and world history are given over to the goal of student "absorption" of a knowledge base; it is why students who only take that one course seldom practice historical thinking. But what if every course, even one at the beginning level, combined some of the narrative presentation of the traditional introductory survey with some of the independent investigation of more advanced courses? Then the student who takes only one history course has the opportunity to learn in the same way that a history major does over multiple courses.[5] Let's examine this approach with reference to my beginning case study of the First World War.

If I were teaching a course on the Great War with the luxury of fifteen weeks to present a narrative, I would spend several weeks each on the long-range and proximate factors leading to war, the parallel experiences on the battle and home fronts, and the aftermath and consequences of the war. But if I allow myself only five weeks for this context setting, I need to condense that narrative. The salient feature of the combat on the Western Front was stalemate. One doesn't have to detail the battles of the Marne, first and second Ypres, the Somme, and Verdun to make that point. What is sometimes referred to as "war pornography" (the one-day casualty reports of suicidal charges into no-man's land, large bits of horses suspended fifty feet up in tree branches, mustard-gassed soldiers leading each other by hand single file like elephants trunk-to-tail in a circus parade) can be presented quite selectively with no loss of impact. Governments entered the war with the venal intent to alleviate domestic problems; any of the problems (the social problem, the woman problem, the Irish problem) can be used to make this point. A wedge of uniquely different experiences was driven between people on the battlefront and those on the home front. This point can be made dramatically by reading excerpts from a chain of correspondence between the front and home (an ambulance driver and her aging father, for example, or an infantryman and his wife), both sides desiring to protect the sensibilities of the other by understating the suffering.

My biggest challenge in the context-setting unit is to avoid making the students feel that they are being rushed or that they are missing something significant. The open dialogue atmosphere of the classroom works here as well. I express my view that a narrative can be taken in at various levels of specificity and in different layers. Just as I developed my understanding of this era by reading many books over an extended period of time, they need to develop a narrative outline and add to it gradually. There is no need for me to monopolize the process of creating the entire narrative when students are capable of doing some of it themselves.

After five weeks of reading, listening to me present a basic narrative of the period, viewing parts of the first great world event captured extensively on motion picture film, and discussing and clarifying their understanding of the era, students have enough background knowledge to begin investigating issues in this historical context more independently. For the remainder of the semester they engage in two extended classroom assessments, each taking up about four weeks. While they continue to read new books and articles on the era as part of these assessments, the emphasis in the classroom is on active application of their context knowledge rather than just adding to that knowledge base.

Assessments replace tests or examinations in our curriculum. Instead of asking students to answer questions in a single sitting about what they have learned after a unit of instruction or at the end of a semester, we ask them to engage in a process of using what they are learning about the historical context to think historically about the evidence of human behavior in this era. Assessment is an extended, multidimensional process, often requiring students to analyze primary and secondary sources individually, then work in groups to multiply each student's effective knowledge base. As a culminating activity, they might write synthetic interpretations and present and defend positions through speeches or panel discussions. Assessment is developmental, with formative instructor feedback on student work at early stages of a project, and the expectation that the students use that feedback to continue to demonstrate their noted strengths and improve in specified areas later in the assessment.

Throughout, student work and instructor feedback are guided by explicit expectations or criteria for effective demonstration of knowledge and abilities. At this beginning course level, for example, one criterion would call for students to group data and draw conclusions according to specific contexts rather than aggregate information about people from different countries or across class, confessional, or gender lines. At this level I would not yet expect students to focus on the perspective of the historian serving as the source of this data, except to insist that students not confuse a historiographical review of other scholars' conclusions with the argument actually being presented by the author of a secondary source. Ongoing self assessment helps students to refine their understanding of these criteria in relation to actual performance, and thereby to use those criteria more effectively as a guide to effective performance. These assessments enable me to measure their ability to think historically in the context of their knowledge of the Great War era and, therefore, to determine whether they have been successful in passing the course.

For the first assessment, students work in groups of four to six investigating the impact of the war on the roles and status of women in various European societies. Each group is directed to work with a library reserve packet of complete scholarly journal articles and selected chapters from anthologies, such as *Behind the Lines: Gender and the Two World Wars,* by Higgonet and her colleagues.[6] These secondary sources examine women's experiences in England, France, or Germany—before, during, and after the war—and supplement students' common reading in a sourcebook of primary documents on European society during the war. Each student selects one of the chapters or articles and prepares a summary, both written and oral, of the author's arguments and conclusions for the other members of her group. They present their summaries to each other, exploring apparent contradictions resulting from the different national emphases and slightly different timelines. The group members formulate a hypothesis about the impact of the war on women—sometimes comparing the experiences in different countries or different social classes, sometimes contrasting gains and losses in different spheres of life—and then proceed over the next two class periods to identify and evaluate specific evidence that will help them argue their hypothesis. The assessment culminates with a videotaped roundtable discussion presented to their peers in the other groups. In preparation for participation in this discussion, each student writes a four- to five-page interpretation of the wartime experience of women, synthesizing what they have read themselves and what they have learned from the presentations by other members of their group. I judge the degree of each student's learning based on narrative interpretation, underlying summary of an individual secondary source, and my observations of the student's participation in planning discussions and the final presentation. I express this judgment in the form of forward-looking feedback, both for continued learning in this course and for development of intellectual skills such as analysis and communication in her other studies.

Challenging Students to Interpret the Past

As inviting as this assessment sounds in principle—the opportunity to explore historical questions independently instead of sitting and taking notes—there are beginning students of history who will not readily seize the opportunity to practice learning through history as I have defined it. In all of our introductory history courses we tell our students that history is not the exact replication of the past; it is the interpretation of the past from the perspective of the historian. But when students are unfamiliar with a particular history, their overriding concern becomes learning what happened. They don't particularly care about the historian who created the narrative they are reading, let alone their own role in interpretation. Our most reliable witnesses to this preoccupation of beginning students are our junior history majors. During an annual meeting between department faculty and all majors entering into advanced level work, our students share with us their experiences in earlier history courses in relation to our intentions and goals for student learning in those courses. They confirm that we made a persuasive and memorable case for historical interpretation and why it is impossible to recreate the past "as it actually happened." But, they tell us, they sometimes just had to set aside the idea of interpretation during the beginning courses. At that point, they couldn't be concerned with the historians' interpretations, assumptions, or motives, because they were preoccupied with finding out what happened. I understand this because I experience common ground with my students every time I find myself in unfamiliar territory, let's say reading for the first time about the Mali Empire in the fourteenth century. Although I interrogate a text with more sophisticated questions than my students, my reading notes reflect a sense of priority for learning as much as possible about what happened and when.

Even though beginning students do not readily recognize the historian behind the history, an assessment such as the one described above can make them aware of at least one act of historical interpretation: their own. If I can block the impulse for students to rely on a single source as a narrative or to find the simplest possible resolution to the assessment problem, they can and usually will recognize their own role as interpreters of history. I do not want my students to experience quick and clear-cut success in answering this question about the impact of the war. The design of the assessment, including the resources I provide them and my interventions at various points, is meant to discourage them from finding a simple answer and to enable them to arrive at the conclusion that they must make choices that are interpretations.

Investigating Complex Resources

All of the readings for the assessment are serious works of scholarship rather than introductory textbook materials. The authors present rich and complex arguments, distinguishing, for example, between pre-war employment opportunities for women in the professions and for those doing wage labor or between the wartime experiences of women of different social classes. Frankly, some of the arguments are too complex for many students at this level to grasp in their entirety. But because students tend to look at these articles primarily as sources of information, they are still able to draw upon them for evidence relevant to their problem. Other students who may already have more highly developed critical-reading skills will be challenged to engage with the historian behind the history.

The set of articles constitutes multiple, overlapping treatments of the effect of the war on pre-war women's progress in France, England, and Germany. The range of article choices and the number of students in each group guarantee that the group will be forced to reconcile at least two studies of women from the same country. If students in their group discussions use the practical principle of corroboration to select only that evidence from two articles that is consistent, and ignore the contradictions, I will intervene and push them to consider the differences as well. Eventually their discussions lead to the sense that there is not a single standard answer to the assessment problem.

Without the structure of the assessment to support students, the difficulty of the task might lead to frustration and prompt some to quit actively investigating. But in this assessment a substantial amount of the investigation takes place in the classroom where other students and I provide support. And the obligation students have to do their best, not only for the sake of their own learning, but for the other students in their group as well, tends to keep them engaged until they finally grasp that they have to take responsibility for making personal, evidence-based judgments about the past.

Decentering Authority in the Classroom

My role in the classroom shifts significantly during this workshop-based investigative assessment. I have to change from the source of expert information (their judgment, not mine) at the beginning of the semester to a coach or mentor who assists them in making judgments for themselves. The critical turning point comes when I roam the classroom listening to (primarily sophomore) students summarizing the arguments in scholarly articles and especially when I read those written summaries after the class session. Obviously, it would be much easier for me to represent the positions in all of the articles myself through a synthetic lecture to the class. I would make far fewer mistakes than my students, and I would ensure that each member of the class had an accurate set of resources as a foundation for the final written narrative. But I wouldn't be assisting my students to practice the discipline. How I correct student error is the key to their growing independence as learners in history.

I correct their readings of the individual articles as unobtrusively as possible, through written feedback or one-on-one conferences in a corner of the classroom. My approach to giving feedback centers on improving the student's reading strategies within the context of the text at hand rather than being based on my greater knowledge of the history. A student may, for example, draw a premature conclusion, taking an opening paragraph literature review that dismisses another historian's position as a representation of the author's own view. In a case like this, I help the student look more carefully at the language, especially words that distance the author from the position being reported. When errors seriously misrepresent the author's interpretation, I tell the student that she must quickly find a way to correct the impression she has given to the other group members. Invariably some students will relay my feedback in the shorthand form, "He told me I got it wrong." This is a critical juncture in the process because if the student got it wrong, then the presumption is that there is a right answer, not merely to the point being summarized from the reading but to the overall process.

Frustration frequently begins to surface here. Students may be thinking, if not saying, "Why doesn't he just tell us what we are supposed to get out of this?" When I sense that, I ask the entire class to consider why I would give them historical problems that were just exercises that I already knew the answers to or answers that could be found completely within any one of the sources. Why would I give them multiple sources instead of just the one best source? I point to their own experiences of reading these sources as evidence that the problem is too complex for one interpretation to cover it all. I also tell them that I expect to learn from this assessment as well. Focusing twenty-five minds on a task, especially when twenty-four of them may have insights into women's experiences that the "expert" does not have, improves the chances that we will arrive at deeper insights about the problem.

Extending the Investigation beyond Empirical Problems

When I notice groups of students limiting the scope of their investigation to a simple empirical question, such as comparing the number of jobs in manufacturing for French or German women ante and post bellum, I will intervene to complicate the problem they are trying to solve. For groups that haven't thought of this themselves, I will ask if they think that the wide-spread layoffs of women and their return to the home after the war meant that the war had made no difference in their lives. Or did a new level of consciousness about what women were capable of achieving indicate progress despite the actual post-war employment opportunities? This is the kind of metaphysical question framing that David Hackett Fischer cautions against in his explorations of the logic of historical inquiry.[7] It is like asking whether an event has a material or an ideal cause. If I were teaching junior and senior history majors to do close analysis of sources, I would not encourage this kind of questioning as a foundation for research because there is no empirical means of resolving this question. For the beginning students in this course, however, it is precisely the kind of question that will keep them engaged in the process of formulating an interpretation, rather than reporting information from an expert source as the solution to their problem. And, of course, the general nature of this question of consciousness raising helps those students who might not otherwise make the connection to see that historical thinking affects our analysis of the present and the future as well as the past.

Learning through History and Civil Discourse

Placing students in a position where they can consider and talk about their own present world through the conceptual lenses of a historian is, for me, what it means to learn *through* history instead of merely learning history. In addition, this teaching strategy is a way for me to fulfill my sense of the historian's obligation to use history to impact present-day society. This is the common ground on which I stand with my students. Especially in the wake of the events of September 11, 2001, my students have used historical thinking to model public discourse that should be taking place more regularly in a democratic society.

For more than twenty years in courses or units on the French Revolution, my students have (to my dismay) frequently questioned the motives and integrity of Maximilien Robespierre during 1793 and 1794. For those not familiar with those two years, the royal armies of most of Europe surrounded France and threatened the nascent liberties promised in the *Declaration of*

Rights of Man and of the Citizen. Robespierre and the rest of the Committee of Public Safety, the legal government of France in 1793, responded to this external threat to the freedom of the French people with a set of security measures designed to strengthen national resolve and to improve the country's actual ability to resist the external threat by cutting down on the distractions of dissent. Collectively this government action was known as the Reign of Terror. It defined political terrorism as the temporary and necessary actions of a government against its own people to promote national security. The suspension of some aspects of judicial due process, the relaxation of rules governing surveillance of citizens, and the general characterization of any dissent as treason were all justified in the name of safeguarding liberty for the future. Prior to 9-11 and its aftermath, very few of my students could fathom a leader dedicated to democracy and civil liberty who would deprive his people of those same liberties.

But after 9-11 and the passage of the USA Patriot Act, all it took was the reminder that, historically, "terror" meant the acts of a government designed to threaten its own citizens with examples of the possible consequences of disagreeing with its policies, and most students recognized the functional relevance of that definition today. They also saw their own experience as a resource for understanding history. Their judgments of Robespierre either became harsher or more forgiving as they compared the Reign of Terror to their own positions on the security safeguards enacted in the United States after 9-11. For most of them in their final speeches on the question of whether human rights can be considered absolute and universal, the balance between liberty and security was not easily determined. It was instead a topic worthy of debate. Whether they criticized the current U.S. administration for violating fundamental principles of civil liberty, exonerated Robespierre for attempting to preserve the possibility of liberty for the future, or judged both situations more tentatively, they recognized that public policy is not the sole prerogative of the government authorities. In a democracy it should be determined by civil discourse. It is too early to tell if the ability to learn through history will become a lasting part of their repertoire of civic thought and behavior. For the moment, however, they are modeling the practice of democracy with more courage and insight than many who have a lifetime of experience in the public arena.

Notes

1. *Ability-Based Learning Program: The History Major*, rev. ed. (Milwaukee: Alverno College Institute, 2001).

2. Sam Wineburg, *Historical Thinking and Other Unnatural Acts: Charting the Future of Teaching the Past* (Philadelphia: Temple University Press, 2001).

3. *Liberal Learning at Alverno College*, 6th ed. (Milwaukee: Alverno College Institute, 2004).

4. *Ability-Based Learning Program: The Psychology Major* (Milwaukee: Alverno College Institute, 1995).

5. James L. Roth, "Teaching Introductory History as if It Were the Last History Course Students Will Take: Strategies and Learning Materials," paper, American Historical Association Regional Conference on the Teaching of History, University of Wisconsin-Stevens Point, November 14, 1981.

6. Margaret Randolph Higgonet, Jane Jenson, Sonya Michel, and Margaret Collins Weitz, eds., *Behind the Lines: Gender and the Two World Wars* (New Haven and London: Yale University Press, 1987).

7. David Hackett Fischer, *Historians' Fallacies: Toward a Logic of Historical Thought* (New York: Harper & Row, 1970).

2

LEARNING TO THINK
MATHEMATICALLY

Susan Pustejovsky

It's the first day of a new semester of beginning calculus. Although more than half of the students are natural science majors and the rest, with the exception of an occasional business or psychology student, are math majors, almost all of them look at me with apprehension. I know their expectations of the coming semester are probably based on experiences in previous math courses. Mostly, their expectations do not match mine. Some of them believe that to enter math class is to enter an alien universe. Others just expect that their tasks will consist of practicing particular ritualistic procedures, after being told exactly what to do. Most students simply do not know that there are ideas involved in mathematics.

I'd like to help students learn that this subject offers them a way to think about questions they are curious about themselves, or that arise in their other studies. How long will it take for a radioactive compound to decay to an amount that is less than 1 percent of what I started with? Is it better to invest my money at 2 percent compounded continuously or at 2.1 percent compounded quarterly? How do I set the price of a commodity to optimize profits? How should the trees in an apple orchard be replaced in order to maximize average annual yield? The list could go on and on, but it takes more than a list of questions to convince students that they can be full participants in formulating problems and devising answers.

For the first day, I hope to help them relax and get interested in the subject. But my hope for the semester is even larger, and I remind myself at the beginning of each new semester that I need to think in terms of what in this course is going to be worthwhile for the students who take it. My goals in this regard are that students will learn to represent ideas that are important and interesting to them, that they will learn that doing mathematics is about "figuring things out," and that they will discover that they themselves can participate actively in formulating and solving problems that connect to their academic and personal interests.

My commitment to learning that is important and interesting to students has crucial implications for the way teaching, learning, and assessment are designed. First, it means that I need to take my students' interests and efforts seriously, because I'm trying to help them engage intellectually with important ideas. Thus we need to begin with some ideas or experiences that are familiar, or to engage in common experiences in order to build on them. For example, on the first day, I sometimes illustrate the concept of "motion events" by walking across the room several times, varying the speed in different ways. I ask students to sketch a graph of my motion. Because there are a variety of ways to do this, many of them reflecting misconceptions or lack of careful thinking, we have an opportunity for discussion. I ask questions about the graphs that are produced, such as "What is right about this graph?" or "How could this graph be changed to make it better?" This is a great way to build on students' previous knowledge about what graphs show; how motion might be represented with a focus on changing distance, changing velocity, and/or changing time; how important it is to be explicit about the quantities one is graphing; and many other issues related to abstraction of observed phenomena in terms of quantities. This activity also introduces a mode of discussion in class that goes beyond simply giving the "right" answer. We spend time discussing what is right and wrong about initial attempts at graphs, thereby practicing a collaborative search for refinement. Many people's ideas may help the group as a whole. Through this simple activity, students have also begun thinking about a paradigmatic idea of calculus: quantifying changing velocity.

In order to emphasize mathematics as a process for "figuring things out," I will have students engage in real problem solving. I need to help them by attempting to make explicit some of the actions they can take in order to successfully solve real problems, and by naming some of the processes and experiences that real mathematical problem solving entails. For example, part of mathematical problem solving is the creation of abstracted representations of the problem. In calculus, this could start with a diagram, leading to the construction of a table of related values or a graph of related variable quantities. Often these representations can act as thinking tools, helping the problem solver make further progress. In this chapter, I elaborate some ways that students in my beginning calculus course practice real mathematical problem solving.

Finally, I design learning experiences so that students not only do mathematics themselves, but also know that they have done it, realizing that they are able to use mathematics as a way of looking at aspects of the world that matter to them. This is perhaps the most difficult challenge for me as a teacher. If I can help them have a successful problem-solving experience, and reflect on the experience, their views about what mathematics is can begin to change. Structured reflection can also help them remember the frustration as well as the positive aspects of engaging in problem solving, so that the affective dimensions are more consciously in front of them, helping consolidate the entire process into an experience that contributes to their confidence.

Real Mathematical Problem Solving

The phrase "mathematical problem solving" can mean many different things. Here, I borrow the definition from the National Council of Teachers of Mathematics (NCTM) Principles and Standards document: "Problem solving means engaging in a task for which the solution method is not known in advance."[1] This statement sets a goal for student learning that is not achieved by simply completing routine textbook exercises or even solving standard textbook problems. If students are to engage in real problem solving, they need to encounter a problem for which they do not already know a solution method.

In my experience, the problem also needs to be real to the student in that she can imagine an interesting question that might be answered through the solution of the problem. Ultimately, real problem solving should have its origin in a student's real question about a situation in which she is involved. However, a beginning learner may not possess the tools, experience, confidence, or imagination to generate and formulate her own questions that can be addressed mathematically. A further difficulty in a calculus class is that students' real questions may not relate to the mathematical ideas and techniques of the course. It seems useful at first to help students focus on particular aspects of problem solving such as producing models for problem situations, or asking further questions about a given problem, rather than on completely unstructured problem formulation.

When I first began teaching calculus to college students, I did not know very much about how to help students with real problem solving. However, I was fortunate to begin full-time teaching in 1991, right in the middle of a sometimes contentious, decade-long national discussion about reforming the way calculus is taught at the college level. Using photocopied chapters from the page proofs of a new calculus textbook[2] designed to support learning problem solving, mathematical modeling, group work, computer exploration, and writing, I gained experience teaching calculus in a way different from the way I myself learned it. I also secured one of the first Internet connections in our office building so that I could participate in ready-made forums and listservs for discussion about student learning in calculus. Of all the pedagogical strategies suggested in the calculus reform discourse, I found that I learned the most about students' thinking by putting them in a workshop setting, in which groups of students worked on activities together, and where I could listen and interact with them as they grappled with ideas, produced mathematical representations, and expressed their ideas.

A commitment to having students engage in real problem solving requires that students spend some class time working on non-routine problems or problems that are not completely well formulated ahead of time. It has been useful for my students to work in groups. The group work in calculus contributes in several ways to a richer problem-solving experience, pushing students to use mathematical representations (tables, graphs, and symbolic expression) with greater care, and creating an immediate need to discuss and write about solutions with precision and clarity. Using class time for problem solving gives me an opportunity to listen in, make suggestions, and give encouragement.

Providing support for problem-solving activity is important because there are affective dimensions to this learning experience that need to be recognized both by the instructor and by students themselves. They may not yet have learned that real problem solving is an experience that won't necessarily be smooth; they will get stuck, they will feel frustrated and confused at times, the process may take a long time and have several dead ends. I can provide support for my students by listening to their ideas and asking questions to help clarify their language and representations. Sometimes I need to suggest actions they can take or representations they can consider in order to further their thinking. I can also simply give encouragement. For many students, it is necessary to help them through the rough spots in order to prevent them from giving up before they achieve success.

In this chapter, I describe two problem-solving experiences I use with calculus students—one for beginning students and one for more advanced students. Included also are the criteria I use to help students conceptualize and organize their processes, and the reflection questions the students answer to self assess their effectiveness as problem solvers. In describing these examples, I wish to illustrate how a carefully planned, extended project can contribute not only to students' calculus knowledge, but also to their growth as mathematical thinkers. Because our mathematics program at Alverno College has a goal of helping students grow into confident problem solvers, such learning experiences must be a part of all course work for our mathematics majors. However, we as a department believe that this experience is valuable to all students in our courses, even those who are not majors.

Two Challenging Problems

One problem I have used with beginning calculus students is the air traffic control problem presented in figure 2.1.[3] Structurally, the problem is exactly like a standard calculus optimization problem (find the time corresponding to the smallest distance between the airplanes), combined with a standard related rates problem (If one object moves at one speed, and a second object moves at a second speed, how does the distance between them change?). However, because the problem is posed outside a particular section of the textbook, and in language that initially requires work to understand, the students tend not to think of it in connection with particular textbook techniques. Instead, they see it as related to other problems of interest, such as the motions of planets or the motion of falling objects.

Instead of working routinely with a textbook template example, the students are faced with figuring things out. The key to finding answers lies in understanding the problem: identifying changing quantities in the situation, reasoning about how the quantities are related to each other, and representing the pattern of changing quantities in some mathematical ways in order to see how answers to the questions might be found. In fact, understanding

Two airplanes are moving along paths toward the control tower at an airport. They are both flying at the same elevation above the tower. Suddenly, the power goes out! At that moment, American Flight 1003 was 32 nautical miles from the tower, approaching from the north-northwest on a heading of 171°, moving at 405 knots. The second airplane, United Flight 366, was 44 nautical miles from the tower, approaching from the west-southwest on a heading of 81°, moving at 465 knots. Your job is to figure out whether the airplanes will pass within 5 nautical miles of each other. In this process, you'd like to answer the following questions as well:

- *At the instant of this first observation, how fast is the distance between the airplanes decreasing?*
- *In general, can you describe the pattern of change in the distance between the planes?*
- *Just how close do the airplanes come to each other? Will they violate the FAA's minimum separation requirement of 5 nautical miles?*
- *How many minutes do the flight controllers have before the airplanes reach their smallest separation?*

To answer these questions, you will need to develop multiple models to represent the situation. Be sure to explain how calculus relates to the solution of this problem, even if you find a different way to solve it. It will help to assume that the airplanes remain at the same elevation (they are not going to land).

FIGURE 2.1

AIR TRAFFIC CONTROL PROBLEM

the internal structure of the problem situation and representing this structure is all that is needed to solve this problem.

A second problem that has challenged students in my more advanced course in multivariable calculus is the roulettes problem.[4] Briefly stated, teams of students use a Spirograph® toy to generate a regular, complex circular pattern on a piece of paper (a path traced out by a point on one wheel rolling along the outside of a second larger fixed circle). Then I challenge them to find equations to generate that same pattern with computer software. Figure 2.2 shows an example of a roulette curve. At the beginning of each project, each student team chooses its own wheel and circle combinations to produce its own pattern, so that each team's roulette is different. Thus, there is no standard answer that applies to all the curves.

The task of finding equations to generate the pattern of a roulette elicits

FIGURE 2.2
ROULETTE CURVE

careful analysis of the internal relationships among quantities. It is quite
challenging, requiring multistep reasoning drawing on geometry, algebra,
and trigonometry. The project further requires students to explain in writing
the derivation of the equations and how they know their equations are correct, and also to ask their own additional question about the problem situation and to find an answer to their question. For example, a student might
observe that different-size wheel and circle combinations result in different
numbers of loops before the path closes on itself. A further question might
be: How does the number of loops in the path before closing change if I
change the size of the rolling wheel?

How do students develop to a level of mathematical sophistication
where they can solve such problems? I believe that having students practice
particular types of mathematical exploration can help them approach even
complex unfamiliar problems. I call these approaches to mathematical thinking *generative,* in that they can be applied in many settings, and the actions
involved lead to mathematical models that will help produce answers to
questions about the problem situation. Many mathematicians have described
similar teaching practices. George Polya, for example, is well known for helping students practice using heuristics in problem solving.[5] For calculus, generative ways of mathematical thinking include the following:

- Identifying quantities in the problem by naming them and their units of measure, and deciding which quantities are changing in the problem and which are not
- Exploring the relationships among quantities with numerical tables
- Making systematic explicit connections between tables of related quantities, graphs, and equations

It is helpful to have students imagine quantities changing. Creating tables and graphs helps them envision quantities changing together. Threefold representation of the problem situation through tables, graphs, and equations and making explicit connections among them promotes flexibility in understanding how to find answers to questions embedded in the problem. An example will illustrate these generative ways of thinking before returning to discussion of the air traffic control and roulettes problems.

Helping Calculus Students Become Problem Solvers

When first acquiring knowledge of calculus concepts and procedures, a student is asked to apply them to solve problems in which a mathematical function represents a relationship between two variable quantities. This central idea of calculus (and of science generally) is simply stated, but not always so easy to see in problem situations. Although students theoretically have had years of practice solving "word problems," often their experience has been limited to "translating" words into algebra symbols and equations, perhaps following a template laid out in a textbook presentation. Some students have had more success with this than others.

Anyone, when faced with a new problem situation, will seek to recognize some familiar pattern. If such a pattern does not present itself immediately, the problem solver will be at a loss. Many students give up at this point. Perhaps their experience has taught them to believe they cannot figure out any new problem by themselves. I believe this is sometimes the case, so as a teacher I need to help the students change their beliefs. Working with students in problem-solving sessions has shown me that sometimes what students need is a set of suggestions about how to proceed when a pattern is not apparent. Practice with generative mathematical exploration seems to be helpful in getting students to start thinking that they can figure things out.

For example, in beginning calculus, it is common to encounter a problem such as the following:

An open-topped candy box is to be constructed from a 24 cm by 18 cm piece of cardboard. This is to be done by removing identical squares from the corners of the cardboard, and folding up the edges to make the sides of the box. Find the dimensions of the box of maximum volume that can be constructed in this way.

The first time students see such a problem, they may not even know that different size squares removed from the corners will result in different volumes. In general, without previous experience with volumes, there is little immediate intuitive knowledge one can use in thinking about the solution to this problem. But one thing anyone can do is to try finding the volume of some different example boxes constructed this way. A small amount of actual experimentation with cutting and paper will lead to a three-dimensional sketch of a box, and can lead a problem solver to construct a spreadsheet-like table of related quantities in the problem, as shown in figure 2.3.

This brief table, which shows only selected values, can lead to much more than just the solution to this problem of finding the "best" dimensions for the most volume. The act of constructing such a table requires identifying quantities in the problem situation and listing, for some concrete values, how the quantities must be related. In fact, each column of this "spread-

Length of side of square cut from corner cm	Height of open box cm	Length of open box cm	Width of open box cm	Volume of open box cm
x	H	L	W	V
1	1	22	16	352
2	2	20	14	560
3	3	18	12	648
4	4	16	10	640
5	5	14	8	560

FIGURE 2.3
TABLE OF RELATED QUANTITIES FOR
CANDY BOX VOLUME PROBLEM

sheet" is a variable quantity, and the numbers in the column are concrete examples of values that the variable can assume. The act of computing one row of this table can lead to the more general observation of the pattern of computations, which can then lead to the construction of algebraic representations of relationships among the quantities.

Many students do not know that an algebraic equation is but one of many choices for representing a relationship between two quantities, and that a table or a graph might prove to be more illuminating or concrete for understanding the structure of relationships within a problem situation. In this example, once the table is constructed, one can easily graph the volume (see figure 2.4 below) as it changes for various choices of one of the other quantities. In this graph, the volume quantity displays a pattern of change across choices for the side of the square, and makes it clear how to find the best choice—look for the highest volume.

The act of constructing a table of values and creating a graph has some cognitive added value. The table enables a person, scanning "down" a column, to understand a variable such as x as a symbol that stands for an actual variable quantity, and to conceptualize it in terms of ordered changing sample values. In other words, reading down a column helps a student to imagine x as a changing quantity. "Reading down" columns in the table corresponds to "reading the graph" left to right. We can then talk about how volume changes as x changes: at first, as x increases, volume increases, but

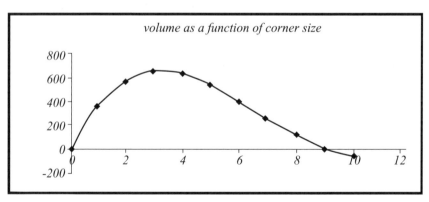

FIGURE 2.4
GRAPH OF RELATED QUANTITIES FOR
CANDY BOX VOLUME PROBLEM

later, as *x* increases, volume decreases. Connecting this descriptive analysis to what the graph shows often provides students with breakthrough insight. Examining the table and graph together helps make both more understandable, and helps reinforce what I tell students is the calculus way of reading graphs: left to right as an abstract display of the pattern of two related variable quantities changing together.

In this way, students practice with flexible and connected use of the representational tools of the discipline (tables, graphs, symbolic expressions) to help think about structural relationships in a problem. Thus, my suggestions for helping students understand the problem include sketching a diagram, making a list of quantities in the problem, and finding ways that the quantities in the problem are connected to each other. All of these are concrete steps that can lead eventually to a mathematical model. These approaches can be applied equally well in more complex problems, such as the air traffic control or the roulettes problem.

Connecting with Research about Good Problem Solvers

The creation of connected webs of knowledge out of discrete data, contextualized practice, and the habit of self-monitoring are all ingredients of expert problem solving.[6] Both the air traffic control problem and the roulettes problem are set up to help students develop in each of these areas. These three aspects, together with recognizing and naming the affective dimensions of problem solving, are necessary ingredients in learning experiences if we are to foster growth in mathematical problem-solving ability.

A description of the air traffic control project will help elaborate the discussion of generative ways of thinking and how self-monitoring is fostered. In my beginning calculus course, student teams work on the project over three days. On the first day, students see the problem for the first time. They are encouraged to use generative mathematical thinking to understand the internal relationships among quantities in the problem. At the end of the first day's work, even producing a numerical table of values corresponding to changing quantities in the problem situation can be viewed as progress. Before coming back to the problem, students complete a brief reflection on this activity, guided by these questions:

- What generative mathematical thinking approaches did you apply to help understand the problem?

- What was your own approach to understanding an unfamiliar problem (work alone first, then talk; or talk to others right away)?
- What were the preferences of the others in your group (work alone first, then talk; or talk to others right away)?
- Did you have an emotional reaction to any of the activities in the problem-solving session?
- What might you do personally to facilitate solving the problem with your group next time?

Students' responses to these questions help me understand each individual better, and help them understand their own process better. Most students report feeling frustrated, lost, or intimidated at first. Some report satisfaction at having made progress with their group. Often, a student can name exactly which idea she contributed that gave her satisfaction. Regardless of what a student says at this point, I can offer encouraging feedback, and point out that she has recognized and named important aspects of her own problem-solving process that she can work to build on later.

On the second day of the project, student teams finish their solution. With encouragement, each group will produce a mathematical model with a variety of representations (numerical, graphical, and algebraic), which they then use to answer all questions. I have found it interesting to observe how generative mathematical thinking suggests ways to figure out the problem. For example, last semester, I heard a student explain to her group that a graph was needed in order to answer the question about how close the two airplanes come together. She had not yet even thought about the details of the graph; she just drew on previous experiences with problems such as the box volume problem to sketch out the image in figure 2.5. Others in her group had questions about this: What is on the horizontal axis? How can we figure out the distance between the two planes? Together, they were able to use her graph sketch as a thinking tool to work out what quantities they needed to calculate in order to produce such a graph. This insight clearly grew directly out of previous work with looking for maxima and minima of quantities in a problem.

The second day's reflection is guided by the following questions, given to students ahead of time in order to help them decide if they are really done:

- Do all members of your group fully understand the problem and your solution, including the process of solution? Did you explain the calculus approach?

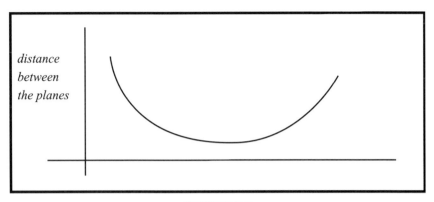

FIGURE 2.5
FREEHAND SKETCH OF GRAPH FOR
AIR TRAFFIC CONTROL PROBLEM

- Have you used multiple approaches to representing your mathematical model (numerical, graphical, algebraic)? Which approach helped you the most?
- Are your mathematics processes correct? How did you check this?

On the third day of the problem-solving activity, student teams write a formal paper explaining their solution. The audience for their paper is another student who has not solved the problem. Writing a formal solution reinforces the idea that the process of mathematical problem solving does not usually proceed in the straightforward, logical way that corresponds to the final written solution. Their written solution gives them essential practice in using precise mathematical language, defining terms, organizing their work logically, and putting the finishing touch on a rewarding experience. Students' written solutions must meet the following criteria, which they then use to complete their written self assessment. The solution must

- Explain the problem
- Explain all representations of the mathematical model (numerical, graphical, algebraic) and make explicit connections among them
- Present results supported by sufficient detail
- Interpret the results in context (i.e., answer all questions posed in the problem)

Since students at this level have had little practice in mathematical writing, it is not unusual for me to require a rewrite. My feedback is most often directed toward helping students explain their thinking at every step: What did we compute or graph or solve? Why did we do this? What do the results mean? Through my support during the problem-solving process, the emotional support of their groups, and feedback, students learn in this project that they themselves must participate in mathematical problem solving, and though there may be moments of confusion or frustration, they can figure out something complex themselves.

The second problem-solving example is one from a more advanced course in multivariable calculus, one that students usually take in the year following beginning calculus. The roulettes project builds on and extends thinking habits that students have developed in previous problem-solving experiences. In order to solve the roulettes problem, students must use all the generative mathematical thinking skills they have previously learned. The first part of the problem is to find equations to generate a two-dimensional curve to match the features of their Spirograph® curve. In order to see how to do this, it is useful to produce a sequence of snapshot diagrams of the roulette tracing process. The act of producing such diagrams leads to the identification and naming of changing quantities, and helps students see that producing a spreadsheet-like table of selected values helps in writing down more abstract equations relating the important variables in the problem.

The relationships are not easy to find, but with the help of my guided questioning, student groups have been successful in finding a set of equations. The work of this project does not stop with the equations, however. The students are challenged with a number of further tasks. First, they need to identify specific features of their roulette that help them know that their equations (tested with the help of computer curve-generating software) really do produce a pattern that matches their roulette. Thus they look carefully at the number of loops before the curve closes on itself, the ratio of the radius of the large fixed circle to that of the smaller rolling wheel, and other factors.

Each group has a different set of equations because each group's roulette is different. The underlying structure of the equations is the same for all roulettes, however, and the students are challenged to express abstractly this underlying common structure, using symbols standing for the parameters, such as radius size. Then, harnessing the power of the computer, they are challenged to ask their own question about other roulettes, and to find an answer to their question. This project is completed over a period of two to three days, depending on how long the groups need to solve the problem. The challenge of asking and answering further questions about the roulette is one that generates a variety of responses, representing progressive depth of thinking.

The last step in this project is to produce a written solution to the problem. The problem has a significant geometric component. Solving it requires use of diagrams connected to internal problem structure and mathematical notation for written explanation. The diagrams and exposition of the solution must be integrated in order that the reader can follow the solution process. I have found that the writing component of this project helps students understand the strong connection between precise written work, use of mathematical notation, and powerful analytic thinking.

The expectation of revision of their paper is built in to the project. Before the student team hands in their first draft, they must verify that the paper meets established collegewide criteria for effective writing, that their mathematics processes are valid and their solution contains a convincing explanation of how they know their equations are correct, and that they have asked and answered a further question generalized from their specific roulettes equations. Student solutions are generally accurate, because the project has a built-in checking process—the computer-generated curve will not match their actual roulette unless the equations are correct. In their written solution, they must elaborate with sufficient detail to accomplish this check.

My feedback addresses the above criteria, and I comment on clarity of exposition and extent of their generalization in asking a further question. Feedback on the first version is quite directive; I give clear instructions about what needs to be accomplished in their revision. Feedback on the clarity of exposition often helps the students think more clearly about the mathematics, resulting in better understanding and a better revised paper. Feedback on the extent of generalization allows me to prompt them to think more deeply about what they did, perhaps to do more exploration, and refine their question to address deeper aspects of the problem. This has usually been the weakest part of the first versions of my students' papers. Students hand in the first versions of their papers with the revisions. The revisions are not complete unless they have addressed every part of my directed feedback.

Student self assessment is based on the requirements of the assignment and the need to address all aspects of feedback. In addition, students are asked to reflect on the problem-solving experience as a whole: their confidence, any frustration, and any special insights they may have had in the process. Many students have reported that they were amazed that they could find a solution to this problem that seemed so impossible initially. Although producing written solutions is time-consuming and difficult for the students, in the end, the process becomes a significant moment in their mathematical growth—they have solved a difficult problem thoroughly, and they know they have done it themselves. It is designed to be empowering.

Our mathematics program is designed to return to these types of experiences throughout a student's course work. It is through such work that students grow to eventually exhibit our department's outcomes, which state that the graduate mathematics major

- Reads, writes, listens, and speaks mathematics effectively
- Uses the language, frameworks, and processes of mathematics effectively
- Formulates and solves diverse mathematical problems and interprets results
- Uses mathematical abstraction

The examples in this chapter show how, within a course, a student can begin to build the skills and understanding that will grow throughout her studies.

Notes

1. National Council of Teachers of Mathematics, *Principles and Standards for School Mathematics* (Reston, Virginia: National Council of Teachers of Mathematics, 2000) 52.

2. David A. Smith and Lawrence C. Moore, *Calculus: Modeling and Application* (Lexington, Virginia: D. C. Heath, 1996).

3. Adapted from Smith and Moore.

4. Adapted from David A. Smith and Lawrence C. Moore, *Calculus: Modeling and Application, Multivariable Preliminary Edition* (Boston: Houghton Mifflin, 1997).

5. George Polya, *How to Solve It: A New Aspect of Mathematical Method,* 2nd ed. (Princeton: Princeton University Press, 1957).

6. See, for example, Alan H. Schoenfeld, "Learning to Think Mathematically: Problem Solving, Metacognition, and Sense Making in Mathematics," in Douglas A. Grouws, ed., *Handbook of Research on Mathematics Teaching and Learning* (New York: Macmillan, 1992).

PART TWO

BRINGING OUTSIDERS
INSIDE THE DISCIPLINES

Donna Engelmann (philosophy) and Zohreh Emami (economics) ground their analyses of their respective disciplines as frameworks for student learning in experiences they themselves had as students of these disciplines. As a result of those experiences, they take a critical stance on what they see as the potential limits of their disciplines, and they consider the implications of their critique for the teaching of their students. They also emphasize how knowing who their students are is central to the teaching process.

Throughout their chapters, Emami and Engelmann address the tension between designing courses in ways that assist students to think in their disciplines and at the same time encouraging them to raise questions about those very ways of thinking. Both also articulate how they design learning that makes their disciplines significant tools for students as they become active and effective citizens.

3

TEACHING STUDENTS TO PRACTICE PHILOSOPHY

Donna Engelmann

Good morning, and welcome to this hearing on the request to open an adult bookstore here in the city. The city council licensing committee welcomes your testimony on this issue, and after your testimony is concluded we will engage in a general discussion of the issues before the committee votes. Thank you for exercising your citizenship in this matter.

After I make this opening statement at the beginning of my final American Philosophy class, my students begin the performance assessment in which they will demonstrate what they have learned in the last third of the course. They have read and discussed a book of essays on pornography, *The Problem of Pornography,* edited by Susan Dwyer, and for the assessment they have selected a role to play from the list I have provided before the assessment.[1] Will they testify from the point of view of an ACLU lawyer, a feminist philosopher, a minister of a local congregation, a young woman working her way through a master's degree program as an exotic dancer? They have already prepared their testimony in written form, and they are required in both their written and oral testimony to draw on the arguments of the philosophers they have read in making their case for or against granting the bookstore a license. In the criteria for the assessment, which I also provide in advance, I specify that their audience is not me or professional philosophers, but ordinary citizens to whom they must make these arguments relevant and intelligible.

How did I come to decide that this performance assessment was the best way to measure my students' learning in the course, and is it effective in providing evidence of their learning?

Part of the explanation for why this is an appropriate assessment lies in the assessment's relation to the learning outcomes for the course. At Alverno College where I teach this course, the faculty have established learning outcomes for every major, and every course in a major has learning outcomes that are based on those major outcomes. This means that students know in advance what is expected of them in regard to demonstrating what they have learned in their major, in every course they take, and in all key assessments. For the philosophy major, one learning outcome is that the student uses the insights of philosophers and other thinkers in developing her own philosophical position.

In the American Philosophy course, a key outcome that reflects the learning expected in the major is that the student use the insights of philosophers and other thinkers in developing her position on contemporary social and political issues in American society. In addition to being required to demonstrate the learning outcomes for the major areas of study, in order to graduate from Alverno each student is required to demonstrate her mastery of eight abilities: communication, analysis, valuing in decision making, problem solving, social interaction, effective citizenship, developing a global perspective, and aesthetic engagement. Courses in the disciplines offer students opportunities to develop and be assessed on the abilities germane to the subject matter. In philosophy courses, we work especially to help students learn to analyze complex philosophical arguments, to relate the values they espouse to the positions and decisions they take, to communicate well orally and in writing, and to perform in public contexts as effective citizens. Hence an appropriate and effective way to measure a student's learning in philosophy and her mastery of abilities would be a simulation that integrates these by asking the student to draw upon the arguments on pornography by philosophers we have studied, to communicate these arguments in a public hearing, and to articulate her own view of this complex social issue.

While Alverno's approach to teaching and assessment of student learning helps to explain why this is an appropriate assessment, other equally important reasons include my encounter with my students and the dialogue with my discipline, philosophy, that has shaped my career as a teacher and scholar. This chapter addresses the questions that arise for me when I consider what to teach of philosophy, how to go about teaching it, and how to assess what my students have learned of it. These questions have been influenced by my experience of being a woman in philosophy, by my experience of sharing Alverno's approach to teaching and assessment, and by considering carefully the lives and learning needs of Alverno students. I believe that "doing philosophy" can be of great benefit to my students personally and professionally, and this conviction is not only shared by my colleagues in philosophy at Alverno, but also captured in the learning outcomes we have created for the philosophy major and for each of our courses in philosophy.

For example, another learning outcome we teach and assess for is that students view the questions and issues of philosophy, not as abstract puzzles only, but as matters of personal and professional significance to them. To achieve the learning outcomes and to help our students gain the benefits of philosophy, my colleagues and I attempt in our teaching to close the gap between our students' lived experience and concerns, and philosophy as an academic discipline. We do this by asking the following questions: What goals do I have for my students' learning (and what are their own goals)? Are my students equipped to practice my discipline, and how should they be prepared for its practice? How can I balance immersing my students in philosophy with helping them to take a critical stance on its content and processes? How can we confront together the excessive specialization of this most academic of academic disciplines? What kind of mentoring will my students require to make "doing" philosophy a lifelong habit?

I have been a teacher of philosophy at Alverno, a liberal arts college for women, for fifteen years, but my relationship with philosophy as a discipline predates my teaching, beginning in my own undergraduate philosophy major. The result of my dialogue with philosophers has been that in addition to developing a particular perspective on my discipline as a political philosopher, I have also developed a critical stance in relation to it. As a philosopher, I am conscious of how women and people of color have been underrepresented in my discipline, and how particular ways of creating and testing knowledge have often made philosophy a kind of competitive endeavor. As a teacher, I see that these aspects of my discipline may cause it to be an alien environment for the women, and particularly the women of color, who are my students. Teaching at Alverno has encouraged me to focus on student learning in my approach and at the same time has provided me with tremendous resources for my development as a teacher.

How My View of My Discipline Has Informed My Teaching

In my graduate work, I trained as a political philosopher, and as part of my preparation I read a great deal in the history of Western philosophy. Although I received my doctorate only a decade ago, feminist philosophers and their works were almost entirely absent from my graduate courses. Without awareness or protest, I accepted that philosophy spoke with one voice, a male voice, and I also accepted that philosophy paid little attention to the concerns of women as women. From the side of scholarship, it was something of a lucky accident that I began to pursue research that led me to explore feminist perspectives. As a political philosopher and a citizen I had long been interested in questions of government authority and citizen dissent. I selected Hannah Arendt's political philosophy and her advocacy of civil disobedience as my dissertation topic, and I began to read feminist political theorists for the first time.

At about the same time, I began to teach ethics to women students at Alverno, and I started to explore feminist ethics in earnest as well. Feminist ethics and politics helped me to understand the ways in which women's experience had been overlooked in the philosophical tradition, and the ways in which traditional philosophizing spoke not only from a male perspective, but also in a distinctly masculine voice. This understanding helped me to analyze some of what was *not* working in my teaching. For instance, when I first taught ethics to undergraduates, I taught ethical theories without providing their historical or social context, and expected students to use them as interchangeable tools for moral decision making. My students were alienated by this approach, which presented the theories as originating nowhere and applicable everywhere. But assuming that traditional ethical theorizing applied to my students' experience was not the same as exploring whether it did or not. I have found that students are more engaged when we get behind these supposed universals by learning together who created the theories and why they were important and useful at the time of their creation. Students are more engaged when I ask them to explain not just how the theories apply to particular cases, but about why they personally find the theories useful and what limitations the theories have for their own analyses. In my ethics course, the goal for student learning, which I am confident I share with most teachers of ethics, is that students begin to develop the ability to make more nuanced and reasoned moral judgments, and to participate in the societal conversation about ethical issues. For this purpose they should be able to recognize and apply the dominant moral theories, but they also need to understand the historical context in which those theories developed, to be able to critique them, and to continue to participate in the evolution of new theories and strategies for practicing ethics, especially those emerging in feminist ethics. Above all, they should be able to gain confidence in their own judgments and voices and be empowered to address issues that most concern them.[2] Many of my students, because they are women of color, feel doubly excluded from the practice of philosophy. My black students do not see themselves reflected in either the history of philosophy or in those who practice it. Of more than 10,000 academic philosophers practicing today, only about 120 to 130 are black. Charles Mills, a philosopher at the University of Illinois-Chicago, has written about this situation—what he terms "the whiteness of philosophy"—and its consequences in, among other works, *Blackness Visible*.[3] Mills insists that philosophy is not only demographically white, but also *theoretically* white. Mills maintains that mainstream philosophers have ignored race in the past, and from a position of social and racial privilege, continue to ignore it.

Although philosophy has been relatively inaccessible to women of color throughout its history, it nevertheless has a great deal to offer them. In *Teaching to Transgress: Education as the Practice of Freedom,* bell hooks writes very beautifully about the liberatory power of theory. She says:

> I came to theory because I was hurting—the pain within me was so intense that I could not go on living. I came to theory desperate, wanting to comprehend—to grasp what was happening around and within me. Most importantly, I wanted to make the hurt go away. I saw in theory then a location for healing.[4]

I see that for some of my students theory can truly be a location for healing, as hooks attests. But while hooks pays tribute to the power of theory in her own life, she recognizes one of its dangers. Hooks speaks in this essay of the tendency for academic philosophy to deem work that is more abstract, full of jargon, and more difficult to read more worthy of attention than work that is accessible to a wider public. In this hierarchy, philosophers who want to speak to their own communities, rather than to address other academics, are disadvantaged. This issue arises for my students and me every day when we try to build bridges between the language and concerns of our own communities and the language and concerns of academic philosophy. And this bridge building is necessary, if students are to achieve the learning outcome for our philosophy program that asks them to view philosophical questions and issues as matters of personal significance. As Maria Lugones wrote in her essay, "Playfulness, 'World'-Traveling and Loving Perception," theorists of color and feminist theorists often find themselves having to travel between different worlds, never feeling really at home in academia.[5] While students cannot recapture in an academic setting the kind of playfulness they exhibit in their home communities, we need to create an environment of trust where they can express their ideas and convictions and try out their voices. These metaphors of "home" and "playfulness" are foreign to the traditional philosophy classroom, however.

In the early days of my graduate work in philosophy, I was struck by how often I was the only woman in my classes. (At that time, it did not occur to me to wonder that there were no people of color.) As the only female, I was proud of my ability to adapt my manner of thinking and style of speaking to the environment—I quickly honed my skills in finding the weakness in an opponent's argument. Right after I started teaching at Alverno, I discovered Janice Moulton's article, "A Paradigm of Philosophy: The Adversary Method," in which she points out that in describing *method* in philosophy we very often speak of a contest of ideas: We find a weakness in an opponent's position, vanquish his arguments, and emerge victorious.[6] Under the control of this metaphor, philosophy is seen as a competitive arena in which the best arguments are tested in intellectual combat, and the truth is the last claim left standing. Moulton laments the effect that this understanding of philosophy has had on its history and practice. Have the best ideas always won? Have some come better equipped for combat than others? Has this contest of truths pushed aside other models of coming to the truth that might be more collaborative and less ego-bruising and alienating?

Some time later I began to read the work of George Lakoff and Mark Johnson on metaphor. In their book, *Metaphors We Live By,* they also point out that our dominant metaphors for argument are based on viewing argument as a kind of warfare where there are winners and losers, and viewing those we argue with as the enemy.[7] What they emphasize is that metaphors have a pervasive role in structuring our thinking and, consequently, our behavior. The metaphors in our language are so deeply imbedded that they are almost invisible to us, and the interpretation of aspects of our lives that they provide seems self-evident and inescapable.

From Lakoff and Johnson, I have learned the importance of bringing to the surface the metaphors imbedded in our language and practice, and analyzing their impact. If the philosophy classroom is always a contested arena, will some students be silenced, will some good ideas go unheard, will the power of collaborative thinking be lost? From my students I have learned that if I were to use relentless criticism of their ideas as a teaching strategy, whether well intentioned or not, it would be demoralizing to them and ultimately drive them from philosophy. Emerging critical scholarship in my discipline has helped to demonstrate for me that there are alternatives to this competitive way of practicing philosophy, and my classrooms have been a laboratory for new ways to do philosophy with my students.

How Teaching Has Influenced How I Think about and Teach My Discipline

When I was interviewed for my position at Alverno College, I was asked a question that took me totally by surprise. I was talking about my previous teaching, and a woman who was later to be my colleague in the Philosophy Department asked me: "What have you learned from your students?" At that point, I was hard-pressed to answer the question, because I believed that the learning relationship goes only one way: They learn from me. Before Alverno, I had assumed that since my students are supposed to learn from me, who they are and what experience and background they might be bringing to the learning situation were pretty much irrelevant. Since then, I have realized that who they are makes all the difference in the world to the way I teach and to whether or not they learn from me.

Knowing Who Our Students Are

At Alverno College, one consequence of taking a learning-centered approach to education is that we begin with the students' interests and capabilities as we find them, and encourage the students' development from that point. We are constantly engaged in a systematic inquiry into the demographics, life experience, and educational experience of students. We must realize in our work with students that even the brightest students need to learn how to engage in and practice philosophical thinking. This means that I must teach students how to read a philosophical essay or construct an argument, rather than assuming that they come to my courses with these skills or that it is up to them to develop them automatically because of the texts they are reading. At Alverno, faculty recognize a collective responsibility to hold high expectations for students' learning, while providing them with assistance in meeting these goals. To have less than high expectations, and not to take responsibility for helping students meet them, would be to abdicate our primary role as educators.

Creating Outcomes for Learning

For my colleagues and me, being learning centered also means creating outcomes for learning for each course and program in the curriculum, including philosophy. We have done so because we believe that students learn better when explicit expectations are established in advance. This helps every student to be a better learner because she is aware of what she is learning while she is learning it. It also helps *more* students to learn; our goal as a faculty is to create circumstances that make it possible for *every* student to learn. At Alverno our experience has been that creating explicit outcomes is an important step in this direction.

The outcomes we have created for the philosophy courses and the program make the requirements for success clear, and we use the criteria for assessment that reflect these outcomes as points of reference for our feedback to the students on their learning. For example, in the American Philosophy course, a learning outcome is that students use the arguments of philosophers in developing their own position on issues in American society. A criterion for the final assessment is that students draw upon the arguments in the readings in the pornography text to support the testimony of the character they have elected to portray in simulation. My feedback to students helps them to see whether they have understood and applied the philosophical arguments correctly and articulated them clearly in the assessment context. In assessing our students' learning, in addition to giving them narrative feedback on their performance, we also ask them to self assess in relation to the criteria, so that they become capable of finding the evidence of successful philosophical thinking, speaking, and writing in their own work. A central aspect of self assessment is the opportunity for the student at more advanced levels of the undergraduate curriculum to set goals for her own future learning; as she matures in our program she takes on more responsibility for this goal setting and takes on a greater role in selecting both topics for study and modes of assessment, given her own learning goals, style, and needs. For example, in the ethics course, students are asked to write a research and position paper on an ethical issue that reflects their own personal and professional interests. I also ask them to create their own learning goals for the course. An example might be a particular goal they want to achieve from among those already established for the major or the course, or it might be a goal related to a development or change in their own habits as a student and thinker. For instance, in recent semesters students have set as goals improvement in their ability to articulate their own views in the face of resistance from others, and setting intermediate deadlines for themselves to encourage progress toward completion of major projects.

Integrating Learning across Disciplines

Focusing on student learning also means that we have as a goal for our students that their lives and their knowledge be enriched by the integration of their learning across many areas, just as our own lives and understanding have been enriched by such integration. We encourage students to articulate relationships among their various areas of study, and try to model this activity for them: Philosophy is not the only thing I do, but my practice of it contributes to every area of my life. And other areas of my life—my roles as family member, friend, and colleague; as lover of literature, the arts, and nature; as enthusiast for politics and community activism—all have enhanced my practice of philosophy.

We model this integration by teaching both within and beyond the boundaries of our disciplines. Because of the benefits to me as a scholar and teacher, I do not see being asked to teach outside my area as a burden but rather as an advantage. Given that the primary mission of my institution is teaching, research in pedagogy is valued for purposes of promotion and tenure as highly as research with a specific disciplinary focus. This has made it possible for me to pursue research in areas both in and outside philosophy, such as civic education, educational and cognitive psychology, metaphor and imagination. I have shared what I have learned in these areas with my colleagues and applied what I have learned to enhance my teaching. I have also extended my teaching competence to include teaching interdisciplinary arts and humanities, communications seminars, and civic education. Teaching in these other areas has given me new insights into teaching philosophy. Teaching interdisciplinary arts and humanities has helped me to have a better understanding of how the content and methods of philosophy relate to the other humanities and arts disciplines. Teaching communications seminars has given me many new strategies for the teaching of speaking, listening, reading, and writing in philosophy. And teaching a civic education course has reaffirmed for me the importance of showing my students how philosophy can be applied to the attempts to understand and resolve social issues.

Collaborating to Foster Student Learning

Thus, being learning centered means not only that each of us as teachers in our own practice models the integration of learning, but also that we collectively commit to breaking down the barriers between disciplines and creating institutional structures that encourage cross-disciplinary collaboration. For example, we are engaged in an ongoing interdisciplinary dialogue about our expectations for mastery of the abilities that each student must demonstrate in order to graduate. During my time at Alverno, I have been a member not only of my disciplinary department, Philosophy, but also of the Effective Citizenship and Valuing Departments. These groups, made up of teams of faculty and academic staff, stay current on the literature about defining, teaching, and assessing these abilities and serve a consulting function for faculty who assist their students to develop these abilities in their courses. As a member of each of these departments, I have developed expertise that has enriched my teaching of philosophy. For instance, I have become more familiar with the literature on teaching moral decision making and citizenship at the college level, and I have benefited greatly from learning teaching strategies for decision making and citizenship from faculty in other disciplines.

Redefining and Promoting Rigor and Excellence in Learning

As faculty in a learning-centered institution, we are valuable to our students not only for our disciplinary expertise, but also for our pedagogical expertise, and for our willingness to be partners with other faculty, staff, and community members, in creating a learning environment that is designed to encourage habits of self-direction, self-awareness, and application of learning in our students. For us, inculcating these habits is at the heart of what we mean by rigor and excellence in learning. Consequently, our classrooms are not so much sites for the delivery of information by teachers to students as they are settings for active and interactive learning.

I want my students to practice, as well as to learn, philosophy. In measuring student learning I use performance assessments such as the simulation in the American Philosophy course rather than using multiple-choice or true-and-false tests, because I am interested in what students can do with what they have learned rather than in their ability to recall isolated bits of knowledge. Assessments may take the form of writing for particular public audiences, group projects, speeches, and panel discussions. As for my role in the classroom, there are very few classes in which "Dr. Donna explains it all to you." I sometimes lecture to set context for learning experiences, to raise new questions, or to prompt deeper analysis, but more often my students work in small groups or large groups to explain texts to one another, to compare responses to ideas and experiences, and to work through problems.

Back to the Questions

So, given all that's been said about the influence of my discipline on my teaching and of my teaching on how I view my discipline, what questions do I ask myself when designing a course in philosophy in a learning-centered curriculum?

> *Setting learning goals: Will the majority of my students become professional practitioners of my discipline or use the insights and processes learned through my discipline to enhance their personal and professional lives? How does recognizing the use to which my students will put their learning change the learning goals and experiences I create for my students?*

The majority of Alverno's philosophy majors will not go on to be professional practitioners of the discipline. Even if they were interested in pursuing the teaching of philosophy at the college and university level (virtually the only occupation open to those with advanced degrees in the field) the personal and economic circumstances of the majority of our students make it necessary for them to be employed immediately after completing their bachelor's degrees. So, as we have designed and refined our philosophy curriculum, we have not had preparation for graduate study as our primary focus.[8] Nor do we feel bound in our curriculum to cover a canon of major philosophical works, "what every philosophy major needs to know." Rather, in our teaching, we select those works of philosophy (as well as works of art and literature) that will serve as effective vehicles for our students to achieve the outcomes we have designated for the philosophy curriculum. The emphasis in these outcomes is on the student using the practice of philosophy to clarify her own worldview and philosophical outlook, developing a questioning response to the world and her experience, and using philosophy as a tool in exercising citizenship in personal and professional contexts. To achieve these learning outcomes, it is important for students to be asked to do something with what they are learning in contexts as close to real-world contexts as possible, and to make links between the community and the classroom. In practice, this means that we depart from traditional approaches in the design of our courses. For instance, our junior-level American Philosophy course is not designed as a comprehensive survey of the history of American philosophy, but as a course in social and political philosophy that draws upon works of contemporary and classical American philosophy as resources for the consideration of current issues. The course is intended to help students to develop an informed and reflective response to social issues and to participate in public discourse and policy making. One requirement of the course (and of all philosophy courses I teach) that helps students make the connection between classroom and community is to complete an individual or group "field trip" to a community event—arts events, public hearings, lectures, and conferences—in which topics related to those addressed in the course are explored.

For example, one semester my American Philosophy students and I attended a public forum on sentencing and incarceration policies in the Wisconsin criminal justice system. For the field trip requirement a student may also choose to interview a professional in her chosen field (since many who take the course are double majors in philosophy and another area or minors in philosophy) to get their perspective on the issues being discussed in the course. Given the goals for the course, the final assessment of the American Philosophy course, which asks students to put their reading of philosophical articles on pornography to use in presenting testimony in a (simulated) public hearing, is the most effective assessment of their learning. Rather than merely a test, the assessment is itself a learning experience that requires students to master and communicate the philosophical arguments we have studied together, integrate several modes of communication, exercise their creativity and imagination, and develop their own views and voices in an interactive public forum.

> *Rethinking the content of the discipline: Do my students see themselves reflected in the tradition or current body of knowledge of my discipline? Are women and people of color absent from the creation of knowledge in my discipline? Are their issues and experiences reflected in that body of knowledge? Are some areas of the discipline more germane to their experience than others? Should I emphasize those areas of my field which are closer to my students' experience, or find ways to close the gap between the remoter aspects of my discipline and my students' lives, or both?*

While it is true that my students do not see themselves reflected either in the demographics or the issues of much of mainstream philosophy, my commitment is to find ways to both bring to them the parts of philosophy that do touch their lives, and to find ways to show the relevance of parts of philosophy that may at first seem remote from their ordinary experience. For instance, in the American Philosophy course, we attend to issues that touch their lives as women, as people of color, as consumers, and as citizens. But we also demonstrate for our students how understanding these issues requires that we explore more abstract philosophical theories of individual and group identity; analyses of gender, race, and class; and epistemological assumptions. We draw frequently on writings of women and people of color, and we situate these writings in their social and historical context by revealing the biography behind the philosopher. We construct the bridge from the students' lives and concerns to philosophy by consistently asking students to relate their own experience to the text and the issues, and to make connections between philosophical methods and theories and their other areas of study.

Their experiences become an additional "text" for the course, as do mine. I share with them my own evolution as a scholar, and the ways in which philosophy has proved liberating for me, assisting me in understanding the world and myself.

> *Rethinking the processes of my discipline: Are my students equipped to practice my discipline? How should they be prepared to practice it? Do the processes of the discipline reflect a particular cultural orientation or set of values? How can I build bridges between the current practice of my discipline and the experiences and values of my students?*

Philosophy teachers everywhere celebrate the role of philosophy in developing the critical thinking and communications skills of their students. I am fortunate to teach in an institution where there is a collective commitment to assist students to develop the analytic, communication, and social interaction skills necessary to be successful at the college level. But the practice of philosophy requires that students exercise specific skills of close reading of texts and argument construction and evaluation. Because many of our students come to the classroom with no prior experience in reading philosophy or constructing a philosophical argument, my colleagues and I have analyzed the level of development of these skills necessary to success in each of the courses in our major sequence. We have created learning experiences that introduce these skills to students and encourage and measure their progressive development. For example, in a beginning course in the philosophy sequence of courses, Search for Meaning, I explain some key differences between the reading they will do in philosophy and the reading they will do in other courses. I supply discussion questions for the readings in advance that direct students to key issues and questions in the texts. At the advanced level, students take more responsibility for analyzing texts in philosophy. They may be asked to generate their own questions for a class discussion, or to come to class prepared to teach their peers the material they have read.

Besides struggling with students' lack of preparation for reading and writing about philosophy, philosophy teachers everywhere also comment on how difficult it can be to engage students' interest in philosophical issues. Rather than sidestepping this problem, I acknowledge to my students that philosophy often seems to be written in a foreign language, a language of a highly educated class of people whose audience is most often other specialists in their field. I address students' disinclination to tackle philosophical texts by consistently highlighting the connection between form and content in the philosophical essays and books we are studying. In this respect, I have learned a great deal about how to teach a philosophical essay from teaching literature. I encourage my students to consider how the rhetorical strategies and language choices in these texts are similar to or different from the choices and strategies they use in their own writing, and how these compare with writing and speaking in other disciplinary contexts they are coming to know. What is the effect on them as readers of the approaches philosophers use, and what can they learn from works of philosophy about explaining their views and persuading others? How does and should the way we communicate change with audience and context?

The issues of engagement extend beyond reading philosophical texts and doing philosophical writing to philosophical discourse in the classroom. How will my students and I find a way to discuss philosophy that substitutes a more collaborative and inclusive approach for the traditional mode of intellectual contest? There are resources within the scholarship in my discipline that open up new avenues for arriving at understanding. For instance, at the beginning of my ethics course one semester, the students raised questions about the role of emotion in moral reasoning. As a response to these questions, I asked them to read Alison Jaggar's article, "Toward a Feminist Conception of Moral Reasoning," in which she describes what she calls Feminist Practical Discourse.⁹ Jaggar views such discourse as it has been practiced among feminist activists as an alternative to the contest-of-ideas model of ethical discussion. In feminist practical discourse, participants do not begin with an articulation of moral rules or principles, but with an account of their own lives, experiences, and responses. Feminist practical discourse encourages the sharing of diverse opinions and discourages adversarial debate; its goal is moral consensus, but the process of sharing and deliberation is prized over the product of a common moral judgment. We have used the model Jaggar proposes both as a contrast to traditional moral reasoning and as a set of guidelines we can use to evaluate our own moral discussions in the course. In this way, I hope my students will be part of developing new metaphors and paradigms for the practice of philosophy.

Balancing in-depth understanding with a critical stance: How can I
balance the need to introduce my students to the knowledge and pro-

cesses of the discipline with the need to help them develop a critical stance on it? How can I help them to know the field in depth while avoiding the danger of uncritical acceptance of the discipline's standards and attitudes? How can I empower them to become agents of change in the discipline?

The last several decades have seen an evolution in academic philosophy in the United States, prompted at least in part by the critique of the discipline contributed by philosophers on the periphery—feminists, third world philosophers, and other philosophers writing from a position on the discipline's boundaries. This evolution has been in the direction of a greater emphasis on applied philosophy and the role of philosopher as public intellectual as, for instance, a survey of the topics addressed in the past decade in sessions at the three annual conferences of the American Philosophical Association would show. The philosophy literature increasingly offers examples of texts that survey the Western tradition while also adopting a critical stance, and it is to this literature that I turn in planning my courses. For instance, in my ethics course I have used a collection of essays, *Applied Ethics: A Multicultural Approach,* edited by Larry May, Shari Collins-Chobanian, and Kai Wong, which offers essays not only by mainstream Western philosophers, but also with feminist, Eastern, and third world perspectives.[10] Working with this literature gives my students a sense of the way the discipline is growing and changing, and the role that women and people of color like themselves have had in calling for change in the field. Encouraging the development of their own philosophical voices in the classroom and in their writing, and accompanying my students to philosophy conferences and other public events where philosophical issues are discussed, also encourages them to see themselves as working philosophers.

Confronting the excessive specialization of the discipline: How are excessive specialization of the academic disciplines, and the jargon and complex rhetoric that are the hallmarks of specialization, a stumbling block for student learning? Do the abstraction and rhetorical complexity of the discipline cause students to feel incompetent to enter the discipline? Do the narrow boundaries of the discipline created by specialization obscure the vital connections among disciplines and the growing permeability of disciplinary boundaries? How can I as a teacher break down the rhetoric and jargon of my discipline to get at vital ideas and processes? How can I show the connections between my discipline and other areas of study?

As I said earlier, I take seriously the responsibility to teach my students the skills of reading, questioning, and arguing necessary to practice philosophy. Our philosophy major course sequence is organized developmentally in terms not just of increasing complexity of content, but also of increasing skill level for dealing with that content. In addition, each course is organized developmentally, with assessments measuring not just mastery of the material we have covered from the beginning of the course to the mid-point, and from mid-semester to the end, but also asking students to do progressively more with what they are learning. This allows students to build competence and confidence over the course of the semester and the program. To bring students into the dialogue of philosophy as practitioners, it is critical, however, to begin this process in the first class, by getting students to respond philosophically from the very beginning, so that they know what doing philosophy is by doing it, not just watching it. They receive both oral and written feedback on the expression of their philosophical views, and the feedback is directed, not merely at finding what is wrong with their writing and thinking, but also at what is worthwhile and solid in their efforts. We try to make connections between their insights and what philosophers have said in a way that validates rather than diminishes their thinking. We also ask them, as in the final assessment in American Philosophy, to translate the ideas of philosophers into language accessible to citizens who are not experts in philosophy, so they experience themselves as having academic expertise to share.

As a woman who is a teacher-scholar in philosophy, I also acknowledge to my students the presence of gender, race, and class bias in philosophy, both where the bias is overt and present in the tradition (such as the many disparaging references in the history of philosophy to women's incapacity for reasoning) and where bias appears in the absence of attention to issues that touch women's lives. I teach my students to be sensitive not only to what philosophers say, but to what they have failed to address.

I work to overcome the narrowness of focus of the discipline by modeling for my students the kinds of connections among disciplines that can enrich the analysis of issues. For instance, what do psychology, sociology, and law contribute to an understanding of the phenomenon of pornography in our culture? I also design assessments, such as the research project that is the final assessment for my ethics course, that encourage students to focus on ethical issues that arise in their areas of professional study outside philosophy, and require them to incorporate insights from those areas of study into their ethical analysis.

> *Taking responsibility for mentoring: Given their learning and life goals, what is my responsibility as a mentor to my students? If they seek a career as professional philosophers, how can I help my students to create a career path which makes the most of their talents and avoids the pitfalls on the way to becoming a practicing philosopher? How was I able to become a scholar/teacher? What information about the culture and practices of the field do I need to supply? Whether or not my students will become professional practitioners of philosophy, what role modeling is required of me?*

Especially if I am preparing my students for the professional practice of my discipline, I must take seriously the responsibility of mentoring them. Faculty in the professional disciplines such as health sciences, education, and natural sciences have done a much better job than faculty in the humanities of taking this aspect of their faculty role seriously, perhaps because the career paths in these fields lead to so many more destinations than research and teaching in higher education. While the possibilities for careers for women and people of color in higher education have expanded dramatically over the last several decades, we have a responsibility to prepare our students who go on to graduate study in philosophy for the competition in graduate school admissions and job seeking created by the limited number of teaching positions in philosophy.

We also have a special responsibility as mentors and advisors to our students who are women of color. Studies have shown that black high-school students are less likely to form interpersonal relationships with teachers and other adults in schools; such relationships encourage success and provide motivation and support for future studies.[11] It is likely that college-age students experience this lack of personal support as well. But whatever their background and goals, an important aspect of teaching students to practice philosophy is helping them to clarify how their practice of the discipline will be a lifelong pursuit. For this reason, another goal the faculty has established for Alverno's philosophy major is that students will articulate how the practice of philosophy will become an enduring part of their lives. We help them to demonstrate this goal both in and outside our classrooms.

In a learning-centered institution like Alverno, no matter what the academic discipline, acting as a role model is a significant aspect of advising. At Alverno, advising is both broader and more specific to the individual student than would be the case in a traditional curriculum. It is broader because teachers see themselves as role models in practicing their disciplines and as coaches for their students, who are apprentices in the field. It is more specific to the individual student, because we encourage our students through the self assessment process to set learning goals of their own and, especially at the advanced level, to make these goals the focus of their study. I am consistently engaged with my students in a dialogue about what they want to learn in my discipline, and how that learning will be put to the service of their career and life goals. The process of self assessment in the curriculum helps them to be more aware of their strengths and areas for continued development, more conscious of how they learn best, and more adept at setting lifelong learning goals. I can build on this self-understanding in advising them about their professional direction and choices.

In mentoring my majors who are considering graduate study, I share my own development as a teacher-scholar and treat the culture of the discipline as one of the topics I am committed to teaching. This sharing and teaching takes place in the classroom and outside it, in individual advising sessions, in informal meetings, and in community events and conferences we attend together. I share, not just information about the field, but also strategies for having a successful and rewarding career.

For my students for whom philosophy will be a lifelong discipline for making sense of their lives and enhancing their professional effectiveness—that is, all of my students—I model the centrality of philosophical questioning in my own life, and I engage them in a conversation about what philosophy means to them. I share the liberating power of philosophy and its role in shaping and resolving my commitments and my perplexities, and what a privilege it is to be able to teach and learn philosophy.

Notes

1. Susan Dwyer, *The Problem of Pornography* (Belmont, California: Wadsworth Publishing, 1995).

2. This seems like a great deal to expect students to be able to do in an ethics course, and it is. However, it is important to note that because our curriculum is integrated, I can count on my colleagues who teach the other philosophy courses to share some of the teaching for these outcomes. They also set theories in historical and cultural context, and help students to achieve a level of understanding that enables them to both apply and critique philosophical theory. Also, because our curriculum is developmental, we teach ethics at the advanced rather than the beginning level, because we believe that the skills and attitudes students need to succeed in a course in ethics are not adequately developed in most freshman students.

3. Charles Mills, *Blackness Visible: Essays on Philosophy and Race* (Ithaca: Cornell University Press, 1998).

4. bell hooks, *Teaching to Transgress: Education as the Practice of Freedom* (New York: Routledge, 1994), 59.

5. Maria Lugones, "Playfulness, 'World'-Traveling and Loving Perception," *Hypatia* 2 (Summer 1987), 3–18.

6. Janice Moulton, "A Paradigm of Philosophy: The Adversary Method," in Sandra Harding and Merill B. Hintikka, eds., *Discovering Reality: Feminist Perspectives on Epistemology, Metaphysics, Methodology and Philosophy of Science* (Dodrecht, Netherlands: D. Reidel Publishing Company, 1983).

7. George Lakoff and Mark Johnson, *Metaphors We Live By* (Chicago: University of Chicago Press, 1980), 4.

8. I want to emphasize, however, that for philosophy majors who do express an interest in graduate study, we make a special commitment through mentoring and offering independent studies to prepare them for graduate programs. This is important to my colleagues and me because we feel that the field needs more women and people of color, who will play a role in transforming the discipline.

9. Alison M. Jaggar, "Toward a Feminist Conception of Moral Reasoning," in James P. Sterba, ed., *Morality and Social Justice: Point/Counterpoint* (Lanham, Maryland: Rowman and Littlefield, 1995), 115–146.

10. Larry May, Shari Collins-Chobanian, and Kai Wong, *Applied Ethics: A Multicultural Approach* (Upper Saddle River, New Jersey: Prentice Hall, 1998).

11. Jeffrey R. Young, "Black Students Have Fewer Mentors in Schools Than White Students, Study Finds," *Chronicle of Higher Education* (January 23, 2003).

4

MAKING ECONOMICS
MATTER TO STUDENTS

Zohreh Emami

The serious student is often attracted to economics by humanitarian feelings and patriotism—he wants to learn how to choose economic policies that will increase human welfare. Orthodox teaching deflects these feelings into the dreary desert of so-called Welfare Economics, a system of ideas based on a mechanistic psychology of a completely individualistic pursuit of pleasure and avoidance of pain, which no one believes to be a correct account of human nature, dished up in algebraic formulae which do not even pretend to be applicable to actual data.[1]

—Joan Robinson

Questions about the causes and consequences of poverty were what brought me to the discipline of economics. As a student from the Middle East I was very curious about the reasons for the wide disparity in income and wealth often seen in societies with abundant natural resources. The combination of a small, extremely wealthy population and a large, extremely poor population in these societies was indeed a puzzle I thought worthy of disentangling.

And what discipline could better help me explore, if not answer, some of these questions, than economics? Getting an education, especially in economics, was a way for me to make a difference by exploring and helping to solve the issues surrounding the persistence of poverty.

Although living in the United States for a number of years did not help me find the answers to my questions, it did lead me to more questions. Having realized that poverty was not confined to the less economically developed countries, I wondered why such a significant portion of the population of the most prosperous country in the world faced poverty. Why did women and people of color bear such a disproportionate burden of poverty? What was the role of education in the alleviation of poverty? And why wasn't economics providing any answers to these questions or at least asking and exploring these questions?

The courses I was taking did not provide the opportunity for asking questions. The theoretical foundations had been laid; the questions had been asked by the forefathers. There did not seem to be any room for debate and disagreement. In my study of the history of economics I read the British economist, Joan Robinson, who was the only economist I could find who had explored what it meant for her to be an educator in economics. In an article entitled "Teaching Economics" she expressed unhappiness with mainstream economics and the way it was taught: "For many years I have been employed as a teacher of theoretical economics; I would like to believe that I earn my living honestly, but I often have doubts. I am concerned particularly for India and other developing countries whose economic doctrines come to them mainly from England and in English. Is what we are giving them helpful for their development?"[2]

Robinson was concerned that those who came to England to be taught became teachers in their own countries, perpetuating the same economics perspectives and philosophy of education that they had learned. "The exam-passer who does well becomes in due course an examiner, and by then he has quite lost any doubt he may once have had to stifle. He has come to believe that this kind of thing really is education. And so the system feeds on itself."[3]

Hoping to enter the conversation among economists, I wrote my dissertation on the history of the theoretical developments on the sexual division of labor and the causes of wage and occupational differentials between men and women, and among different ethnic populations. This dissertation topic in the history of economics afforded me the opportunity to study the spectrum of ideas in economics on these topics and made me understand the relevance of historical debates on contemporary conversations and policy prescriptions. I was struck by how the economics profession had excluded the contributions of women to the discipline. I discovered feminist research, not part of the mainstream economics education of students in the United States, that argued that women's invisibility was the result of a systematic exclusion of feminist scholarship. While mainstream economists argued that women's individual choices had led to the collective lack of scholarly ability and output on the part of women, feminist research demonstrated that women's theoretical contributions were either attributed to their male contemporaries or simply ignored. Feminist researchers documented the ways in which women had been denied tenure, promotion, and the opportunity to publish.[4]

Mainstream economics has defined economics as the science of individual choices involved in the allocation of scarce resources. Some feminist economists have defined economics as the science of provisioning needs.[5] These economists have pointed to the significant economic value of women's traditional responsibility for the unpaid work of caring for dependents in the context of an economics defined as the science of need provisioning.[6] Women's caring labor, on the other hand, has contributed significantly to the economic dependence of women on men and therefore to the economic disadvantage of women in an economy arranged on the basis of a theoretical perspective that defines economics as the science of individual allocation of scarce resources. My study of feminist economics led me to questions I might not have been encouraged to ask otherwise, and the questions have informed both my thinking about the discipline of economics and how it can be a framework of learning for my students. How much has the exclusion of women's contributions to the meaning and definition of economics had to do with the lower wages and occupational segregation of women and people of color? What has been the effect of this exclusion on the public policies our societies have designed to tackle these problems? What would it take to level the playing fields?

As historians of economics, Paulette Olson and I interviewed twelve contemporary women economists, in part to gather their evaluations of the discipline.[7] Almost all complained about the discipline's increasing irrelevance as it has become more abstract, theoretical, and mathematical, and less policy oriented over time. Many considered economics increasingly exclusionary, insular, and resistant to alternative perspectives. Heterodox economists, who are on the margins of the discipline, argued that economics is essentially hostile to historical and institutional analyses since this kind of work is considered subjective and unscientific.

I had come to economics with a desire to be an active participating member of society, making a difference by exploring the causes and cures for social and economic inequities and thus helping to contribute to the well-being of the less privileged members of society. The theoretical emphases in mainstream economics and the way it was taught, however, did not encourage me to question its assumptions nor to apply my learning to issues with which I was most concerned. In fact I was being taught very explicitly in my studies that economics is value free, that ethical considerations have no place in the scholarly considerations of the economists, and that any aspirations for purposeful amelioration of social ills by economists, or anyone else for that matter, are at best wishful thinking and even dangerous. It was as if economists had discovered the truth, and there was no point in dialogue and debate.

From the perspective of a student from an economically less developed region, I was struck that I was not being asked to study questions of growth and income distribution that were relevant to the countries in those regions. I was asked by mainstream economics to take the resources in those countries as given, essentially to assume equitable distribution, and simply to investigate the question of the distribution of these given resources among alternative ends. I was inspired by the questions Robinson was asking:

> If the serious student has the hardihood to ask: but are the resources given, and is income distributed equitably? He is made to feel foolish. Do you not understand that these are necessary simplifying assumptions for the analysis of prices? You cannot expect to do everything at once. It is true that we cannot, in the time available, teach everything that we would like. But why do we pick out for treatment just that selection of topics that is least likely to raise questions of fundamental importance?[8]

I was drawn to Robinson because she sympathized most directly with the students from the developing world who studied mainstream economics, since she saw this perspective as completely irrelevant to the issues faced by these students and their countries. Yet, as time went on I realized that she saw the problem of irrelevance of mainstream economics as a more general one stemming from its ahistorical reliance on equilibrium analysis and its presumed applicability to all people everywhere.

It was in the context of this experience with economics that I became a teacher of this discipline at Alverno College, a small, liberal arts women's college, with a history of scholarly research and practice in teaching and learning. Alverno serves a diverse student population, 38 percent of whom are women of color and 75 percent of whom are first generation college students. The most important thing I learned at Alverno was that education goes beyond knowing to being able to do what one knows. There was a legitimate reason, after all, for being distressed about not knowing what to do with what I had learned in economics. I also learned that if the teacher is to take the doing of a discipline by students seriously, it is imperative that she start with where the students are, what they bring with them, their hopes and aspirations, their fears and misgivings. Exactly the opposite had happened in my own educational experiences. I had had to learn to ignore where I was coming from, my aspirations and values, in order to be accepted as a student of economics.

Moreover, I came to see that students learn better through active engagement with a discipline, an approach quite different from what I had encountered in my studies. Learning is more effective when it involves interaction between the student and the teacher, among the students, and with the environment and society. In this sense the needs of the individual learner, the needs of the societies students come from, and the nature of the conversations of the disciplinary community—within both the orthodox and heterodox perspectives and between them—are all dimensions to be explored and considered. The teacher and the learner become collaborators in the learning process. Providing opportunities for students to explore their questions given their individual circumstances, helping students formulate further questions, and engaging students' imagination are all parts of this collaboration. Finally, I learned that learning endures if it is relevant and transferable to circumstances beyond the classroom. After all, what good is an education if the only time it is applicable is when the student is in the classroom? Being able to use what one has learned in multiple contexts—refining, expanding, and evaluating one's learning—is what being educated is all about. This is when I realized that disciplines can be dynamic and living, their application conditional on the specificity of circumstances, and changing as they are learned, taught, and relearned.

Teaching, Learning, and Relearning Economics

My relationship with the discipline of economics changed dramatically as a result of being in an environment where teaching was taken very seriously and where I was considered first and foremost an educator with economics as my context. Looking at economics as a collection of disciplinary frameworks through which I could help students become educated opened up for me a brand new approach to the discipline.

I teach women, many of whom are first generation college students, who are quite diverse in background, and who range in age from eighteen to seventy years. At Alverno we do not have economics as a major, although we have beginning, intermediate, and advanced level courses in economics as requirements and electives for majors related to business, community leadership, and global studies. As a result, I find myself teaching a varied group of students, most of whom come to their beginning economics courses at best unfamiliar with or not interested in the discipline, or at worst absolutely dreading it. Interestingly, even those who come to our economics courses with some background in economics have some of the same reservations about economics as heterodox economists. For instance, they cannot identify with the atomistic individualism of mainstream economics and its emphasis on the pursuit of self-interest. The overly abstract, formalistic approach of the discipline also contributes to its irrelevance in their eyes. The sophisticated student, in the advanced levels of the curriculum, is sometimes critical of the universalistic tendencies of mainstream economics, its claim to have an explanation for everything and its neglect of its own history. It is amazing how smart students can be!

While understanding and appreciating my students' sometimes skeptical attitude towards economics, I believe that economics can be a helpful discipline in many ways. It is imperative that women participate actively in economic analysis and economic decision making both on the personal and familial levels and at the level of national and global conversations and debates regarding social-economic policies. Ironically, although women are in fact significantly affected by economic decisions that are made both at the microeconomic and macroeconomic levels, the number of women participating in these debates as professionals or even as informed citizens is relatively low. In other words, decisions are being made for women in which they don't have much say. Moreover, many of my students and their families make significant sacrifices in order to get educated and often feel a strong sense of responsibility to give back to their communities as competent individuals. Being able to make well-informed economic decisions is a necessary condition of their overall education.

I have attempted to deal with my understanding of, and even respect for, my students' lack of interest in my discipline on the one hand, and the significance of their participation in economic decision making on the other, by continually exploring with them, with my colleagues at Alverno, with colleagues in higher education in general and economics in particular, and with professionals outside of higher education, what it means to be educated in the twenty-first century. What should an educated person know and be able to do at this time in history? What should students know and be able to do in economics? What do students need to know and be able to do in economics if they are not majoring in it? How should the needs, responsibilities, hopes, and goals of my individual students figure in what and how I teach them?

Knowing Who My Students Are

I hope it is clear by now that knowing who my students are is an important first step in helping them learn effectively. Knowing who they are involves not only understanding their demographic backgrounds, but also understanding and helping them develop as individual learners. As I mentioned earlier, they are often not excited by the prospect of taking economics, so my first strategy is to get them engaged. My approach to getting them engaged in economics is to start from where they are. At the beginning stages of their development as learners in economics, I try to find out who they are, what ideas they bring with them, what they already know, what they think economics is all about. Developing a conversation surrounding these issues also emphasizes from the start that dialogue is an essential vehicle for learning. In order to start this conversation I ask students to read various local newspapers and to talk to people in their communities. They identify economic issues that affect their lives and come up with a definition of economics. We discuss these in small and large groups in class. The point is to give everyone a chance to explore with others what significant economic issues are, how these issues affect their lives, and what, therefore, the definition of economics as a discipline should be. Students are very unsure of themselves at this stage, and the message I intend to communicate to them is that each and every one of them has a voice and that a key purpose of this course is to develop that voice. In this process they also begin to understand the importance of listening and collaboration in their learning.

I have struggled considerably with this dimension of my teaching because I was trained to think that my job was to deliver knowledge. Letting students talk and taking them seriously when "they don't know any economics" at first made me feel I was shirking my responsibilities as a teacher. It wasn't until I realized that the whole point was their learning and that engaging their interest was necessary to my success in helping them learn, that I felt comfortable with letting go of what I thought was my responsibility to deliver content. After all, the point of teaching is not the discipline per se but the student's learning of the discipline.

Learning to Question

Starting with students' prior knowledge is my initial strategy in order to engage them, but keeping them engaged is another challenge. I have come to consider the development of the students' ability to ask questions as uniquely important to continuously engage them. In order to facilitate my students' development of the ability to ask questions, I believe that they need to explore the historical context of economic conversations and debates. The historical contexts for theories create intellectual organizational mechanisms for students that help them understand, internalize, and use economic discourse. A historical approach helps students view economic theories as social constructions and problem-solving frameworks for tackling social questions. For example, in studying the rise of market economies, they explore the questions that faced the social/political/economic thinkers of the time (economics as a stand-alone discipline was not born until after the rise of market economies). Asking themselves what questions societies were faced with in the transition period to market economies often has them identifying the question of how order can be reestablished in a formerly paternalistic society increasingly conceptualized as the interaction of self-interested individuals. Approaching economics historically helps students to analyze the relevance of theories and to connect economic theory to economic reality. They learn to ask themselves about the questions society was asking, is asking, and should be asking. They learn to wonder why these questions are being asked and not others. They can explore what is being said as well as what is being left unsaid. They can ask whose values are represented in specific theories. I have found that being able to ask questions puts into their hands the tools for making economics relevant. It is a way for them to connect history to the present.

Developing the ability to ask questions is difficult, because it is so open-ended. You have to think for yourself, you have to understand what others have said, you have to have heard the various voices in specific controversies, and you have to consider multiple perspectives. For example, in the context of studying both the history of economics as well as contemporary economic debates, students learn to ask about the historical roots of the contemporary debates surrounding the role of government in the economy. They explore the question of whether present conditions warrant the application of the perspectives relevant in the past century or the past decade. They consider the ways in which economic life has changed and the ways in which economic circumstances have remained the same. They ask questions about the changing role of government in the economy and anticipate the consequences of policies implied by alternative perspectives. Developing the ability to ask probing questions is empowering. It draws upon the student's analytic, global-perspective-taking, and valuing abilities. The assumption inherent in this approach is that students are entitled to inquire and to explore and that economic phenomena are subject to continual investigation—that the final truth has not been discovered.

Developing the freedom to ask questions helps students to enter the conversation from where they are and to explore the questions they come with. In this context students have the opportunity to evaluate contemporary theories in light of their own values. They can judge the relevance and realism of theories in helping them understand economic phenomena and in making decisions about social, political, and economic issues. They learn to explore the strengths and weaknesses of specific perspectives. Moreover, through questioning they can explore the relationship of economic analysis to other disciplinary explorations and judge the worth of interdisciplinary integration. By bringing together their learning in philosophy, history, sociology, political science, and economics, students learn to ask about the values inherent in various policy debates and the social arrangements reflecting these policies. For example, they often ask about the importance of freedom versus justice in social, political, and economic practices.

The Developmental Nature of Learning

A foundational assumption at the heart of the teaching and learning process at Alverno is that learning is developmental, so I design courses with the students' developmental level in mind, creating learning experiences that do not assume advanced level proficiency, but that provide students with the opportunities they need to develop. In the early stages of their learning in economics I generally provide more structure and direction, while at more advanced levels I expect that they can begin to operate more independently as learners. This developmental approach is important in the sequence of learning experiences within a course as well as in the sequence of courses themselves.

At the introductory level, in a course on the economic environment, the process I use to develop my students' questioning ability and to assess their progress is a series of debates. As the students explore the history of economic thought and of the economy, they engage in structured debates. We do the same with contemporary issues. I have found that students understand and internalize the tenets of this history as well as contemporary policy and can retrieve the relevant dimensions of their knowledge of economics if they are actively engaged in exploring, arguing, and questioning. I have found that one of the most significant dimensions of their ability to question is the development of their ability to evaluate theories. As we know from being teachers, asking meaningful questions is not an easy task. The students engage in many hours of practice in the process. The following is one example of how I facilitate beginning students' engagement in the discipline of economics.

In the beginning course on the economic environment, before the students' knowledge and abilities are developed, I assign specific economic perspectives for each student to defend and question, and I provide a fairly structured format for the debates. For example, students debate the role of government in the economy and are either assigned to represent the neoclassical perspective, arguing for a minimal governmental intervention in the economy, or the Keynesian perspective, defending the significance of the government's role in market economies. As the course progresses, the students start developing well-informed opinions, and they can begin to dialogue with their peers under less structured and more independent circumstances. This course often culminates with each student writing an editorial for the Alverno student newspaper on a contemporary economic issue of the student's choosing, in which she informs her peers about the various dimensions of the issue, analyzes the conversations surrounding the issue, and provides her rationale for a particular policy prescription, point of view, or position. Given the significance of the debate surrounding school vouchers and public school funding in Milwaukee and in many of the students' home communities, for instance, many students apply economic perspectives in exploring this issue in their editorials. Other favorite projects are the debates surrounding environmental protection as well as various antipoverty programs.

In preparation for the debate the students develop questions for both sides of the issue. They spend considerable time individually and in small groups posing questions, evaluating each other's questions, and answering each other's questions. By acting as the questioner in the initial debates, I assist them in coming up with fundamental questions about the underlying values that guide individual decision making and human societies. I model for them what appropriate questioning is in the context of a debate. I want them to learn to ask why there are multiple explanations for the same phenomena. How do different people explain the causes of these phenomena? I help them explore the kinds of communities they live in. I expect them to ask themselves about the kinds of communities they aspire to live in. My goal is to help them ask the questions they have and to develop the questions they didn't know they had or might not have considered before. Students begin the questioning process by simply asking themselves and each other essentially clarification questions. We identify these as questions of clarification, work on answering them, and move on to evaluative questions that ask how the perspectives we study could or would answer questions that address inconsistencies, value conflicts, relevance issues, or major contradictions. In the context of probing the Keynesian perspective, for instance, students often ask about how Keynesians would respond to critiques that would argue against government intervention because of its tendency to reduce work incentive. Students often want to know how the neoclassical perspective, with its emphasis on individualism, allows for the provisions of needs for the poor and the infirm.

Throughout the course I evaluate students' learning and give them feedback on how to continue their learning. I spend considerable time giving feedback to students on the probing quality of their questions and their understanding of economic theories. I am especially interested in how their questions have been informed by their understanding of the theories they have studied. The students also give each other feedback on their performance in the debates. In other words, each student has a role to play in every debate: debating, asking questions, or giving peer feedback. Each student also engages in ongoing self assessment in which she reflects on the development of her abilities and what continues to challenge her. Reflecting on one's intellectual development, observing oneself in action, seeing patterns in one's abilities, making judgments about specific performances, and planning for the future are habits that need to be taught and learned; they take time and practice.

It is worth emphasizing that the assessments in this course—the debates, written and verbal analyses of the debates, the questions, the editorial, and the self assessments—are all opportunities for evaluation and for further learning. They are key performances in which students identify significant dimensions of specific situations, apply what they have learned in appropriate contexts, demonstrate their ability to observe patterns in economic analyses, and evaluate multiple perspectives. Throughout these assessments the students' performances are evaluated on the basis of explicit criteria. Students are always made aware of the intended learning outcomes and the criteria used for their evaluation. For example, during the initial debates I look for the students' ability to articulate basic patterns that explain the history of economic thought and to make logically consistent connections among economic theories, their value foundations, and the role they assign to government. Later on in the course, I look for the students' ability to make relevant connections between contemporary theory and the history of economics, to select pertinent economic theory to analyze economic problems, and to make balanced judgments in taking a position in the context of contemporary debates.

These assessments often include varied opportunities to demonstrate analytic, problem-solving, and valuing abilities in the context of economics as well as the opportunity to rethink and revise. They can be quite challenging because they require students to have developed cognitive organizational mechanisms necessary for internalization of knowledge; to be able to retrieve appropriate knowledge when necessary; to integrate various abilities; and to communicate through effective reading, listening, speaking, and writing. Assessments, therefore, require performances that can be quite complex, requiring a grasp of the subject at hand and the ability to use it effectively in given contexts.

The extended example I have just provided illustrates how I design learning and assessment within an introductory economics course. Not only are individual courses designed developmentally at Alverno, but the curriculum itself is conceptualized with the developmental nature of student learning in mind. In an advanced level course in international economics for students in global studies and international business, I work on designing experiences for students that develop their ability to ask questions at a more advanced level. In this course the students are engaged in a semester-long research project on a country of their choosing from the perspective of a member of a non-governmental organization (NGO). This serves as the primary assessment of student learning in the course. All our readings on theories of economic trade and development, the debates surrounding globalization, the history and role of international organizations, the debates over philosophical underpinnings and value foundations of various measures of economic activity and well-being are sources for asking questions relevant to the research project. Each class session of four hours is devoted partly to small group discussions of the readings in the context of the questions students pose, and partly to each student using what she has learned about the readings from the discussion to enhance her research. She makes connections for herself and her fellow students among the concepts, theories, and questions under consideration and the specific country she is researching. For example, when reading articles on the impact of globalization, the students explore the relevance of the various perspectives for and against globalization for the specific economy they are researching. They explore the application of various definitions of economic well-being—for example, the growth of Gross National Product versus the Human Development Index—in these economies. Students learn not only to explore the relevance of alternative perspectives on different countries, but also to inquire how various peoples in each country are affected as a result of global economic developments and policies. For instance, they often ask about the degree to which any country has the right to bring pressure to bear on another country to change its practices and what form this pressure should rightfully take. They often wonder whose rules regarding labor and the rights of women and minorities should apply in the construction and implementation of economic agreements. Each class then ends with the discussion of further questions and considerations that have emerged as a result of the attempt by each student to apply the readings to the circumstances of her selected country.

The work students do in this course is challenging advanced level work that helps them use economic theories in independent ways. The students start developing their expertise in a specific country early on and enter conversations about economic theory, policy, and practice as developing experts. They learn firsthand the conditionality of economic analyses—that the same truth is not applicable in all circumstances. They also discover that a one-size-fits-all solution to the problems facing various countries is not possible and that solutions often depend on the kind of questions asked. In this process they learn, sometimes slowly, to feel more and more comfortable in dealing with complexity and ambiguity. In fact, some students start believing that they themselves can make contributions to the development of economic knowledge if they develop their expertise.

Learning to foster the open-ended nature of student learning involved in this ongoing assessment has been a challenge for me too. Even advanced students are often quite uncomfortable with the messiness of asking substantive questions and applying economic theory to specific circumstances. There never seems to be a perfect one-to-one correspondence between economic theory and economic reality, and this frustrates students. In fact, I see one of my main jobs as stressing this ambiguity of economics as a framework for learning. It is sometimes difficult to resist the easy route of simply teaching theory without worrying about asking students to get their hands dirty and apply it. I have had to learn to help students deal with their frustrations. I have had to think seriously about what it means to help undergraduates start developing their expertise through reading economic literature and asking substantive questions. I have had to work with students to help them develop intellectual organizational mechanisms, such as broad thematic outlines of historical and contemporary economic perspectives, that can help them retrieve what they know at appropriate times. We have all had to work on developing the intellectual and emotional flexibility and maturity required for students to be able to transfer their learning. I have had to help students understand the social construction of theory while at the same time avoiding radical relativism.

In International Economics, after finally coming to terms with the extent of the theoretical and policy controversies in economics, students want to know why they should debate things that cannot be resolved. Initially they wonder how we can discover an ethical anchor to guide policy formation once we recognize the presence of such deep ethical discord. It often takes a while before the students learn to adjudicate among potential policies and outcomes based on ethical disputes and to maneuver in the context of the social turmoil that value conflict can often induce. The epiphany for students often comes when they realize that being shut out of a community's ethical debate is to be substantially disenfranchised.

When analyzing global policy regimes and their outcomes, students learn to ask whose values and norms should guide the formation of such rules. They ask how we should think about the difficult matter of the construction of institutions, rules, and norms that shape global economic relations in a heterogeneous world marked by distinct cultures, competing inter- and intra-cultural accounts of the right and the good, alternative religious and secular doctrines, and so forth. What authority should be taken to supersede others, when different people and societies invoke different objectives? What are we to make of the groups and even entire societies that we deem to have gotten it wrong?

Arriving at this point often leaves the student with a whole new set of dilemmas. Exploring the problems of essentialism and reductionism associated with moral objectivism leads students to ask if there is much that can be done in the face of poverty and inequality in the absence of an unambiguous set of objective moral principles. They ask how we can resist and replace monological international policies of conflict for the dialogical politics of respect and compromise in a world where different people hold to different objectivist accounts. How can the cultural relativist virtues of promoting cross-cultural understanding and respect be reconciled with the objectivist tendency to promote a certain basis for action and resistance?

As their teacher it is my hope that my students' questioning of the epistemological claims of moral objectivism does not engender in them an "anything goes" attitude. Recognizing that our best judgments in our present context of time, place, and culture are the only means we have to implement change might help us exhibit a bit more humility in our decisions, recognize our earlier errors, and open us to learning from others. But it would be a mistake and an abdication of responsibility to refuse to consider, judge, and act, all because we lack certainty. When ethical conflict is explicitly or implicitly suppressed either through the imposition of a code of ethics or through the uncritical acceptance of one, a critical aspect of democratic practice is sacrificed. Learning to engage each other in open, fair, and meaningful debates and dialogues is the essence of self-governance in a democratic society and, thus, is at the heart of my approach to teaching economics.

Notes

1. Joan Robinson, "Teaching Economics," in *Collected Economic Papers of Joan Robinson*, 3 vols. (Cambridge: MIT Press, 1980), 3:2.

2. Ibid., 3:1.

3. Ibid.

4. Mary Ann Dimand, Robert W. Dimand, and Evelyn L. Forget, eds., *Women of Value: Feminist Essays on the History of Women in Economics* (Aldershot: Edward Elgar, 1995).

5. Julie Nelson, "The Study of Choice or the Study of Provisioning? Gender and the Definition of Economics," in Marianne Ferber and Julie Nelson, eds., *Beyond Economic Man* (Chicago: University of Chicago Press, 1993), 23–36.

6. Paula England and Nancy Folbre, "Contracting for Care," in Marianne Ferber and Julie Nelson, eds., *Feminist Economics Today* (Chicago: University of Chicago Press, 2003).

7. Paulette Olson and Zohreh Emami, *Engendering Economics* (London and New York: Routledge, 2002).

8. Robinson, 3:3.

PART THREE

TEACHING THE COGNITIVE PROCESSES OF THE DISCIPLINES

Perhaps not many students, or faculty, for that matter, would identify chemistry and English as similar disciplines in terms of the learning frameworks they provide for students. In these two chapters, however, Lucy Cromwell (English) and Ann van Heerden (chemistry) ask very similar questions about the way they approach the teaching of their fields. Indeed, van Heerden begins her reflections on chemistry by recalling her experience teaching English to teenagers in Botswana.

The heart of both chapters is an articulation of the kinds of thinking that the authors see as characteristic of their respective disciplines. The authors also consider the challenge of how to articulate those ways of thinking most meaningfully and effectively for their students. In addition, they describe the pedagogies they have developed with their colleagues to engage students in the practice of the disciplines, and they describe assessment processes they have designed to evaluate student learning and give feedback for improvement.

5

READING AND RESPONDING TO LITERATURE

Developing Critical Perspectives

Lucy Cromwell

. . . all of literature is part of the same dream
and one of the few pleasures allowed us on this
earth.

—Gabriel Garcia Marquez[1]

Some twenty-five years ago, I addressed a group of our graduates at commencement and encouraged them to think about what it means to be considered a "literate" person. I challenged them to think beyond the idea that being literate meant that they were skilled in language use or that they belonged to an educated elite. I wanted them to reflect on the specific role that literature played in their education and, I hoped, in their lives. I told the graduates that I believe that the study of literature is a major way in which we come to understand the human experience; I said that literature gives us a sense of the world around us, of human nature, and of events, that even experience itself cannot give.[2] My hope for the graduates was that they would continue to read and explore the way that literature expands their understanding of the world. In the intervening years since that graduation address, I have not changed my high opinion of the role of literary study. I have, however, become more systematic in my approaches to teaching literature in order to provide better opportunities for students to learn.

Now, when I consider the role of my discipline in a student's education, I think—as do many educators today—about what I want my students to know, and what I want them to be able to do because they have studied literature. My colleagues in my department and I have come to the conclusion that students who study literature learn to think and feel in unique ways. My purpose here is to examine the ways that the study of literature develops students' minds, and to discuss teaching and assessment strategies that promote this development.

Defining Literary Study

Our approach to teaching literature at Alverno College is based on the learning assumptions of our ability-based curriculum, and it is also a response to the ongoing national discussion of the structure of the English major.[3] Although there is a centuries-old tradition of studying literature as a history of what was written and the styles in which it was written, more contemporary explorations of the English major are much more likely to look at the interplay between the way literature represents reality and the way it shapes and controls it. Attention to the individual reader's involvement in the work, responses, and ways of reading also plays an important role in course planning and development of assignments. By asking students how they come to think about their reading in their particular ways, we encourage an examination of both the literary work and the thinking process of the reader.

In our department, we think that studying literature is a multifold process: Literature is the study of specific artistic works, of literary genre and form, of human history, and of human experience. Additionally, the study of literature is the study of aesthetic response—that of the individual reader, and that of the wider culture. In the intersection of all these concerns are the thought processes that hold it all together.

Students who study literature at Alverno College develop approaches to learning and thinking that come specifically from the interplay of literature and life, of knowledge and ability, of text and perspective. Like other scholars in the field, we have considered the way that the creative and artistic aspects of literature affect the critical side of the discipline.[4] It is certainly a defining characteristic of our discipline that we analytically critique works written through a creative process. While many writers refuse to explicate the "whys" of their creative process, we English professors routinely infer process and meaning, and we expect students to do so as well. This relationship between the imaginative and the analytical is exciting, but it can be frustrating, especially for students. If we do not provide students with the tools to read both imaginatively and analytically, they can feel, as many readers do, that literary understanding is a mysterious skill known only to the initiated.

As instructors, we systematize the reader's role by evaluating the validity of students' responses. Often, we expect students to have a particular kind of response, either in a general reading reaction or in answer to specific questions that we ask them. I don't mean that we have a precise answer in mind, but rather that we think that students will come to their reading with certain tools and assumptions. We may expect, for example, that students will assume the writer is creating an imagined universe that may function on its own terms rather than ours. Or we may expect that students will assume that the motivations of the characters are not to be confused with those of the writer. Or we may anticipate that students will consider the historical context of the work as part of what shapes their response. Or we think students will "see" the same themes in a work that we do. When there is a discrepancy between our expectations and student responses, both we and the students can become frustrated. Many students have told me that they became so frustrated at not getting the "right" answer that they lost interest in engaging a literary work that proved to be challenging or difficult. As our department has reconceptualized our goals, expectations, and strategies for teaching and assessing students, we have reaffirmed our belief that students who study literature can learn to think in ways that allow them to enjoy the imaginative qualities of literature, write and speak about the work from a variety of critical perspectives, and feel confident that their responses are based on the relationship between their unique reading experience and the more systematic world of critical reading.

Ways of Thinking about Literature

In this chapter I hope to show how studying literature develops a particular way of thinking. Specifically I want to discuss how reading, and analysis of that reading, help to create a mind-set that allows for the interplay of imagination and analysis, between the created and the real, between the random and the patterned. By examining the stated outcomes we have developed for our students and the way those outcomes shape our courses and assessments, I hope to show that a student can develop a "literature mind-set." Students who learn to think through the study of literature often tend to be open to multiple viewpoints; they tend to let a situation offer ways to interpret or understand rather than imposing one view on things. They develop a world-view based on openness rather than conclusions. They learn to look for relationships and connections; they learn to let the patterns they infer help them understand things. Looking at the world from a background in literature study is an inductive way of responding; it is an attempt to infer patterns in experiences, to negotiate between the imaginative and the real, and to see how each affects our interpretation of the other.

Can a student be successful in the study of literature and not respond to the aesthetic wonder that literature presents to us? I sincerely hope not, not if we define success as an awareness of the relationships between storytelling and reality, between form and meaning, between chaos and order, between imagination and analysis. Our challenge as teachers is to state our departmental outcomes in order to create a structure that continually allows the student to consider not only the subject matter of her courses, but also her personal and intellectual interpretation of what she is studying.

Certainly one of the goals of studying literature is to read and come to know some of the "great" works of our past and present. But this knowledge of the artifacts of our discipline is only the beginning. Of course I want my students to be well read, to know the literary tradition. But I'm just as concerned that they develop a sense of the role of literature in our lives. This concern with the role of literature puts our attention on the way storytelling plays a major part in human life.

The Function of Storytelling

Storytelling is a basic human activity. It isn't just the writers—great or merely average—who tell stories. We all do. Each time we tell someone about an experience, or recount an event from the past, or explain our life history, we are telling stories. We focus on certain aspects of our "story," highlighting some things and eliminating others. Sometimes we choose to eliminate details; other times we do it unconsciously. We create a tone for our story. The same event can be told as a humorous anecdote or a serious calamity, depending on the way we shape it. And we tell our stories with particular purposes, sometimes consciously and sometimes not. We aren't always aware of our biases or the way memories can affect what we remember or think we know. Listening to siblings tell stories about their shared childhoods often reveals very different versions of the same experiences.

Helping students to become more aware of this human tendency to tell stories is a way to bring them into the art form of literature. It is a way of making the artifice of a novel or story more meaningful to them. I have found that students are more likely to become engaged in reading a work—even one that is difficult for them, or distant from them in various ways—if they have thought about and internalized certain concepts of storytelling.

In an introductory general education course in integrated humanities, for example, students begin their study of literature by considering their own experience of growing up. They write an essay explaining an insight they had about the adult world and how they realized what they had learned. After this personal consideration of the idea of "growing up," they read "The Lesson" by Toni Cade Bambara. In this story, a twelve-year-old girl and her friends are taken by an adult to an expensive toy store. The woman who takes the children seems to want them to realize that they don't know much about the world or the economic realities of their impoverished background. Some of the children are angry when they see things they can't have; others say it isn't fair. Sylvia, the narrator, seems to reject the lesson, and yet—in the context of the literary work—she is the one who remembers it most, "telling" it as an adult, long after the fact of the trip. In their humanities course, my students deal with this story as more than a reading exercise. They make connections to their own thoughts about what it means to grow up and learn the realities of life, and they make interesting connections between the way they wrote about their experiences and the way Bambara presents the character Sylvia's experience.

Analyzing the way that Bambara uses the perspective of the adult voice presenting her younger self, the somewhat humorous and crass language of the young children, the multiple responses to the toy store visit, and the lack of a stated "message," gives my students a number of important issues to consider. Why doesn't the author tell us what to think about the children's experience? Why does she write in a vernacular and seemingly careless language? Why does she make Sylvia seem so resistant to learning the lesson that Miss Moore, the teacher, is trying to convey? Why do we as readers see the lesson when Sylvia refuses to?

All of these questions deal directly with the way that literary study affects the way we think. A careful reader moves beyond the literal language and asks about deeper meaning. And a reader attuned to literary conventions begins to look for connections and patterns. Beginning students sometimes have to set aside their preconceived ideas about literature. They may have to reconcile their assumptions about "literary language" with an author's creative use of slang or even of language that some might find offensive. Perhaps they confuse the author's personality with that of the narrator or main character. A particularly difficult task for some students is to move beyond the plot of a work to consider the way that style and structure also convey meaning. In other words, the so-called literary way the story is told is as much a part of the meaning as are the events in the story. The pleasure we receive from reading a well-crafted story depends very much on an appreciation and understanding of the patterns and relationships we discern, or to which we intuitively respond. This is the ability that students sometimes see as the "secret messages" that only English teachers are privy to.

Thinking within Literary Frameworks

This ability to analyze the writer's use of elements and also to respond to and consider the writer's themes is precisely what we believe literary study can teach students, and it is one of the hallmarks of thinking within literary frameworks. It is the ability to make inferences based on one's own experience with the world and yet to base those inferences on the imaginative work of another—the writer. There's an old saying that life is stranger than literature, because in literature everything has to have a purpose and make sense. That may not really be the case, as contemporary writers continue to break the established rules about literary unity, but there is certainly a way in which the metaphoric world of literature offers as much "truth" as does the external world we all live in. Students of literature become adept at reading with close attention to detail and providing evidence for their inferences.

Many teachers of literature would agree that what we want from our students is not necessarily a "correct" response, but rather a response based on careful attention to the literary evidence provided—through tone, language, metaphor, character development, theme, and so on. So in a significant way, one of our main objectives in teaching literature for beginning college students is to shake loose some of their fears about being wrong in their responses to their reading. What we have attempted to do in our approach to literary study at Alverno College is to assist students systematically to develop abilities to be open to new styles and unique forms of expression, to build a repertoire of critical approaches and frameworks, and to continually deepen their involvement in literary works from the traditional canon and outside it. We have done this through development of a curriculum that spells out student outcomes for our courses and through attention to the use of critical frameworks in all our courses.

In explaining how we came to structure our English curriculum in the way that we did, a number of significant things should be pointed out. Our English curriculum has been affected by our relatively small size—seven full-time faculty, with approximately forty majors and some eighty minors. Interestingly, however, we have discovered that what might have been seen as a drawback actually led to a strength of our program: We created a developmentally progressive set of courses. We needed to find ways to make our courses coherent, to ensure that each course would be a significant part of the whole picture. We didn't have the luxury of offering many choices in a given semester, and we needed to find ways to raise the bar with each level of course so that students would see that their study of literature was becoming deeper and more complex as they progressed through their requirements.

Creating a Coherent Curriculum

Another factor we needed to consider was the relationship between our English curriculum and our collegewide ability-based curriculum. For each of our courses we identified the key abilities that students work toward, and the developmental level toward which they should strive. Attention to this ability focus made us consider how our courses would build upon each other. Our challenge was to ensure that courses provide opportunities for and demand increasingly more complex and sophisticated ways of reading, talking about, and examining literature. It would not be enough to have more difficult or more esoteric reading lists and literary selections; the nature of the course and the quality of the students' experience would have to be different as well.

In the process of creating a curriculum that addressed the challenges of small size, limited course offerings, and a collegewide focus on abilities, we defined departmental outcomes that would be meaningful to students while they were in school and also later in their professional and personal lives. We sought to solve our dilemma of appropriate course content and level of assignment through collaborative efforts, and we strengthened our focus on student development by carefully considering what we wanted students to do with literary study—and how we would teach them to do it. We defined departmental outcomes.[5] A student majoring in English at Alverno College shows progress in the following outcomes throughout the curriculum:

- Reads and interprets diverse cultural expressions in works of literature, film, and other media
- Communicates an understanding of literary criticism, questions its assumptions, and uses its frameworks to analyze and evaluate works
- Collaborates in aesthetic communities by articulating how literary studies affect professional choices and public life
- Writes coherently and creatively, making conscious and sophisticated stylistic choices in language and structure
- Engages personally, intellectually, and creatively in the expanding discourse of the discipline of English

The way in which students learn to demonstrate these outcomes changes and deepens as they work their way through our curriculum. Our courses are developmental, both in terms of genres and literary canon, but, perhaps more important, in terms of what students learn to do.

In beginning courses, students read primarily for the "story." They show understanding of the characters and give some sense of how they might relate to the characters. Students can point out literary elements such as symbol, or narrative point of view, but they generally do not make connections between style and theme, for example, or explain how a particular narrative point of view affects the way a reader gains insight into the plot or theme. Students exhibit discrete skills, not yet integrated with each other in a systematic way.

In intermediate courses, students learn to be more systematic. They go beyond analysis of discrete elements to make connections and infer relationships. They learn the components of several significant literary frameworks and use these frameworks in responding to and analyzing several works.

They work more systematically with patterns—including doing analysis in groups—to show how different people do close reading and how it affects individual responses. They move further into the "conversation" of reading and responding to literature.

In advanced courses students bring together discrete pieces of literary analysis and response and learn to infer patterns from their reading. They are not content with isolated observations about their response; they learn to make connections and see how they are building interpretation. They do not work with an "imposed" pattern, but learn to infer appropriate approaches themselves. They develop the ability to let the work suggest possibilities of meaning.

Examples from Literature Courses

Some examples may help show how students deepen their abilities to interpret and respond to literature as they progress and how they develop their own communicating and thinking abilities. In an initial English course, we have designed learning experiences that will encourage our students to consider their personal responses to literature and to examine the way writers make artistic choices as they create their works. Although we are teaching literary analysis at a beginning level, a major focus of the course is on the concept of imagination. As I have indicated earlier, I believe that a distinguishing characteristic of thinking "like an English scholar" is the awareness of the connection between imaginative and analytic approaches to a literary work.

In an introductory experience in this course, I ask students to use these ways of thinking in response to a very short story, "The Continuity of Parks" by Julio Cortazar. I read the opening segment of the story aloud to my class. The story presents a man returning to his estate after settling some legal affairs in the city. He sits down in a green velvet chair and begins to read a book. As he reads, he becomes captivated by the story he is reading—a pair of lovers are meeting to plan a crime. As the first paragraph of this very short story closes, the lovers part, and the male goes off to perpetrate the crime. At this point, I stop reading and ask student to discuss their reactions. They quickly begin to speculate on the plot. They surmise that the lovers are going to kill the woman's husband, and then they turn to the primary plot of the man reading the story. It doesn't take long for students to question the connection between the two narratives. Their previous reading experiences have taught them that literary works generally have unity and understandable connections.

I ask students what they think will happen in the rest of the story. Always, someone in the class has suggested that the lover is coming to kill the man who is reading the story—even though common sense says that the two narratives are occurring on two different planes of reality. I read the rest of the story: The man reading in his room reads on—he reads that the lover comes quietly up the drive to an estate, enters the house, and stops behind a man sitting in a green velvet chair. Cortazar stops his story here, but we as readers have many issues to discuss. Students look at significant details of the plot (which I have not detailed here) and are especially drawn to the detail of the green velvet chair that ties the two narratives together. I ask students if the story is plausible and, if not, where something like this could make sense. They usually conclude that this could happen in our imagination. For readers not experienced with literary conventions and the idea that writers can manipulate our sense of reality, this is an "aha" moment. For students it is often a pleasurable sensation to realize that they have participated in an imaginative experience.

Throughout the semester in this course, I ask students to respond to their reading in both analytic and imaginative ways to build on this initial sense of enjoyment and achievement. I give students response assignments that focus on a particular literary element that we are studying, but I often do it through a creative assignment. For example, in analyzing characterization in Edith Wharton's story "Roman Fever," I ask students to consider the ending of the story, through the following writing assignment:

> Wharton's story, "Roman Fever," ends with a startling revelation, but it does not provide us as readers with answers to some of our questions. How might each of the two women feel now that they have revealed such significant things to each other? And does Wharton prepare us as readers for the "surprise" ending?

> Imagine that you are one of the two women, and that you have gone back to your hotel room after your emotional meeting with your old friend. Write a journal entry in which you think back on your fateful lunch, exploring how you feel about what has happened.

Before I used this assignment, I often had students complain that the story ends too abruptly, that they didn't understand what secret seemed to have been revealed, and that the two main characters didn't seem distinct from one another. By asking them to take on the persona of one of the two women and, writing in the first person, to respond to the events of the day they have spent together after a twenty-five year absence, I have found that students analyze the personalities of the women and look carefully at what happened many years ago to precipitate the shocking revelation at the end of the story. Students come to understand Wharton's presentation of character development, and they—again—have a satisfying literary experience as they apply their imaginations in an effort to understand Wharton's literary creation.

In another assignment in this course, students give an oral presentation, taking on the role of a guidance counselor trying to explain the actions of a disturbed young girl in Joyce Carol Oates's story "Stalking." Again, my previous experience with the story had been that students were disgusted by the young girl's destructive behavior but didn't always go beyond that to see the complex picture that Oates has created in the story. By "entering" the story, my students analyze character development, setting, symbol, and theme as they look carefully at Oates's bleak picture of a lonely teenager in an affluent wasteland.

By the end of the semester in this beginning course, students have written new endings for stories, explored the use of symbols in their own lives, rewritten stories from a different literary point of view, and generally immersed themselves in the imaginative worlds of the stories they read. As the semester ends, the assignments become more and more analytic, so in a final assessment students write a "traditional" essay analyzing their interpretation of the theme of a story. Students work with stories that have not been discussed in class, so they show that they can apply their learning in a new reading situation.

Applying Critical Frameworks

Although the assignments I have described engage students in the imaginative side of literature, they also serve to give students practice in applying critical frameworks as they read. Students in this beginning course work within the formalist framework as they examine the way writers use the literary elements of the short story form, and they practice within the reader-response framework by exploring connections between aspects of their own lives and their understanding of the works they read. In the next level of courses in our English curriculum, students specifically learn about the way critics read and analyze from the perspective of specific analytic frameworks, and they practice applying some of the key frameworks to selected novels. As teachers, we hope that students will continue to respond creatively to their reading through their imaginations, but at this level of course we become more systematic about the use of frameworks. To that end, we assign a textbook that explains literary theory, we have students read critical essays about literary works that they are studying, and we ask them to develop their own critical stances about their reading.

In her chapter on the humanities in *Learning to Think: Disciplinary Perspectives,* Janet Donald states that "the most useful truth a student can learn . . . is that a piece of literature yields different insights depending on the questions put to it."[6] This idea is at the heart of our intermediate-level course, Practicing Literary Criticism. In other words, there are no specific or "right" answers to be found in literary analysis; it all depends on the approach one takes and the questions one asks. Students learn the assumptions and methods of four critical frameworks: formalist, reader-response, historical, and feminist. Certainly they have already had some isolated experiences with these frameworks in previous courses, but now they study them thoroughly, and apply them through reading, writing, and speaking assignments.

In this course, students build on the reading skills they developed in their beginning courses. They complete close reading assignments of their texts. For example, they annotate the opening pages of a novel, taking note of language, images and metaphors, themes, and so on. Over a period of several days, they return to the close reading and add to it any additional insights and observations that occur to them. In a written reflection they relate their observations to the reading of a chapter of Steven Lynn's text on criticism, *Texts and Contexts.*[7] Here is their assignment:

> As Lynn explains in his first chapter, carefully noting your responses to a text is a fundamental element of reader-response criticism. He suggests asking yourself some key questions as you read:
>
> • How do I respond?
> • How is an ideal or implied reader "supposed" to respond?

- How does the text shape these responses? That is, what expectations does it create? Are they fulfilled?

Using these questions as your guide, analyze your close reading and discuss what it suggests about your expectations for the novel.

This kind of close reading of the text can serve as the basis for other kinds of work, as in this later analytic assignment for Anne Tyler's *Ladder of Years*:

Select one of the patterns you noticed in the first half of the book [through a close-reading assignment]. Write a report on the way the pattern is carried out in the second half of the book. Does the pattern intensify? Change? Combine with other patterns? Disappear?

In your first paragraph, introduce the pattern you are following. Then, give several examples of the pattern, especially from the second half of the book, to test out how the pattern develops. Conclude by examining what this pattern does for you as a reader.

In this assignment students work with the idea of observing an author's writing process and making inferences about the patterns and relationships they see. They use their understanding of the formalist framework to gain insight into the overall structure and meaning of the novel.

Throughout this course students are directed to use specific analytic frameworks—we are "imposing" the approach rather than allowing students to select their approach. We believe that this directed approach helps students develop the systematic approach needed in careful literary analysis. In their advanced courses they become the initiators of the critical approach, but here they are guided and given opportunities to practice specific approaches. This practice prepares students for a final assessment, based on Toni Morrison's novel *Sula*. Working in groups, students role-play members of a school board charged with considering *Sula's* suitability as a high school text. As my colleague Carole Barrowman writes of this experience, "This particular English assessment demands that students practice a high level of critical thinking, including the ability to summarize, synthesize, draw relationships among differing ideas, and take a position from those ideas that will serve them well in any workplace. Students also leave this course with an appreciation for good literature and the critical theories that have grown from it."[8] The imaginative and analytical again come together in this process.

Students continue to develop their abilities to do close reading in other intermediate courses as well, learning how to do careful annotation of texts and determining a sense of themselves as readers. For example, we ask students to make a formal presentation to the English faculty in which they show a photograph that presents a metaphor for the kind of reader they are. This challenge to think of themselves metaphorically (and visually) has yielded wonderful results. Student metaphors have ranged from a detective searching for answers to a traveler who uses books as traveling companions, to an inexperienced boater ready to tip over her rowboat, for example. By exploring their sense of themselves as readers, our students show progress toward our stated goal of "engaging personally, intellectually, and creatively in the expanding discipline of English." They analyze patterns in their own responses; they expand their repertoire of critical frameworks; they depend less on faculty-assigned approaches and become more independent in their choice of framework and perspective.

Advanced Courses

When our students reach their advanced courses in our major, we as teachers expect them to have integrated the critical approaches and the learning strategies they have learned thus far. We ask them to read significant texts from British, American, and world literature and, now, to infer which critical approach will yield insights that they will want to share with their teachers and their peers. The level of involvement and expectations is raised again, and class assignments reflect increasing complexity. Something that demonstrates both the collaborative and the systematically analytical nature of our students' experiences is the way in which several faculty members ask students to take on a teaching role in their course. In my course on major American authors, for example, groups of students are required to involve the class in a consideration of a specific author or work. Students are responsible for a teaching function for the class. This means that they conduct a portion of the class—in whatever way they think will be valuable for the class's learning. A major consideration should be how to involve the rest of the class in some kind of hands-on, or minds-on, activities. The criteria that I provide students for this group lesson show how open-ended, and yet focused, the assignment is:

- Shows understanding of the author or work presented
- Deals with a significant aspect of English study
  - consideration of an analytical framework
  - exploration of one or more literary elements
  - dealing with genre issues
  - critical response to the work
  - readers' response to the work
  - comparison/contrast to other works/authors studied
  - placing work in historical and literary context
  - etc.
- Involves students in a learning activity
- Shows creativity in planning/presenting lesson

Students take this challenge seriously, and they create lessons that are attentive to critical frameworks but that also involve imagination and creativity. For example, one group presented a formalist study of Emily Dickinson's poetry by creating poetry strips of Dickinson's work and asking the class to create new poems using random strips of lines. Dickinson's views on love, nature, death, and family emerged vividly. Another group measured off and taped on the classroom floor a footprint of Thoreau's cabin at Walden Pond as they led the class through a study of what they would take with them to "live deliberately" as Thoreau attempted to do. Each lesson was just one part of our weekly class session, but the personal involvement and imaginative consideration of the literature provided memorable experiences. It is gratifying to note that students created the imaginative approaches to the works themselves. I may have given them specific creative exercises in their beginning classes, but now they were able to infer appropriate ways to approach their specific literary work or author. At the end of this teaching component of their assignment, students were required to write an essay that would be suitable for publication in a formal collection of college writing.

Involving Students in Their Discipline

Our English curriculum requires students to complete a series of benchmark assessments in which they create, annotate, and update reading lists of the significant works they have studied. They arrange—and rearrange—their lists by interest level, by genre, and by historical period. Finally, they write a self assessment that examines their achievements and explores their goals for the future. Our students become engaged in the processes inherent in being thinkers in English. It is gratifying to see that other scholars and teachers are also calling for more systematic approaches to involve students in their discipline.

Recently, for example, Elaine Showalter challenged humanities programs to consider pedagogy as well as content in a serious attempt to deal with the scholarship of teaching. She particularly addressed literature faculty to "find new ways to help students learn how literary scholars think, read, analyze, annotate, evaluate, and interpret texts."[9] Our experience with students in our courses and our curriculum attests that when students are asked to analyze and respond to their reading in ways that represent the thinking strategies of literature, they not only read more attentively, but they also become more aware of their own responsibilities as readers. They go beyond summarizing others' ideas about a text, and they provide evidence from their own experience and from careful scrutiny of the literary work.

In another discussion of English curriculum, explaining his department's curricular redesign at Montclair State University, Lawrence Schwartz concludes that, "Above all, our goal is to enable our students to join us as careful, appreciative readers, incisive writers, critical scholars, scholarly critics, and fully engaged conversationalists."[10] I applaud his statement, and I think it summarizes our goals as well. By articulating departmental outcomes that are based on our best sense of what it should mean to be a professional in our discipline, we have developed courses, learning experiences, and assessments that reflect what we do as English scholars and how we think about our discipline.

So how do students of literature confront the world, as a result of their learning? We have found that our students become adept at considering that many perspectives come into play in any situation. They realize that the perspectives they hold—or choose—affect their conclusions. They learn to step outside themselves and realize that their personal responses and experiences affect the way they read and interpret. They know the implications of their perspectives: that they must be especially careful to provide evidence for their ideas, evidence that comes from careful observation and inference making. They understand that language and metaphor can show us ways of understanding that are every bit as powerful as so-called "reality." They see reading and interpretation as dynamic and changing processes; they learn that creativity and imagination can be powerful ways of thinking. And, if they are lucky enough to fall under the spell of literature, they realize, as Marquez says, that literature is one of life's great pleasures.

Notes

1. Gabriel Garcia Marquez, quoted in Francisco Goldman, "In the Shadow of the Patriarch," *The New York Times Magazine* (November 2, 2003), 41.

2. Lucy Cromwell, "Cromwell Commencement Speech," *Alverno Today* (Winter-Spring 1979).

3. The members of the English Department at Alverno College work collaboratively and share ideas and teaching strategies. I thank my colleagues for their part in the design and implementation of the courses and experiences I describe in this chapter: Carole Barrowman, Mimi Czarnik, Jonathan Little, Georgine Loacker, Robert O'Brien Hokanson, and Judith Stanley.

4. Janet Donald, *Learning to Think: Disciplinary Perspectives* (San Francisco: Jossey-Bass, 2002).

5. *Ability-Based Learning Program: The English Major* (Milwaukee: Alverno College Institute, 2002).

6. Donald.

7. Steven Lynn, *Texts and Contexts: Writing about Literature with Literary Theory* (New York: Longman, 1998).

8. Carole Barrowman, "Improving Effectiveness by Defining Expectations," in Elizabeth A. Jones, ed., *Preparing Competent College Graduates: Setting New and Higher Expectations for Student Learning*, New Directions for Higher Education, No. 96 (San Francisco: Jossey-Bass, 1996).

9. Elaine Showalter, "What Teaching Literature Should Really Mean," *The Chronicle of Higher Education*, January 17, 2003, *The Chronicle Review*.

10. Lawrence Schwartz, "The Postmodern English Major: A Case Study," *ADE Bulletin* 133 (Winter 2003).

6

ARTICULATING THE COGNITIVE PROCESSES AT THE HEART OF CHEMISTRY

Ann van Heerden

I learned how to "think like a chemist" through nine years of education and three research positions. I thought about what that means, though, only when I became a teacher. My discovery of how chemists think has evolved largely because of my interactions with students. I have come to believe that this discovery is absolutely critical for effective teaching; it has impacted my courses, my relationship with students, my pedagogical approaches, and my assessments of students' performances. The following is the story of this discovery, some of my findings, and the implications for my teaching.

Internalized Cognitive Processes

When I was a Peace Corps volunteer, I tried to learn Setswana (one of the official languages of Botswana) from a Motswana (a citizen of Botswana). I remember the frustration of finally understanding some grammar rule only to find out that there were many more exceptions to the rule than cases that actually followed the rule. One time when we learned a phrase that seemed to violate all the grammar rules we had ever learned, my fellow classmate asked, "O itse jung go re jalo?" which translates to something like "How do you know to say that?" Kagiso's answer was, "The tongue knows." Her answer, of course, didn't help us out at all since our tongues *didn't know*.

A month later I was in a classroom in a little village in Botswana facing thirty teenage children who were bravely trying to figure out how to speak English, their third language. They wanted to know why they couldn't say, "I'm going too, amn't I?" I resisted the urge to say, "Because that sounds funny," knowing that would be no more helpful to them than Kagiso's answer was to me. Instead, I had to figure out what set of rules and exceptions and patterns I use every time I speak, even though I had long ago internalized them.

I had a surprisingly similar experience my first year at Alverno College teaching a freshman chemistry course. My students had just spent a couple of weeks learning how to determine the bonds that hold together simple molecules (like water and carbon dioxide and hydrochloric acid) and how to represent the structures of those molecules in figures on paper. In preparation for their written assessment on chemical bonds, I gave them a quiz question to do in class. I pointed out to them that H_2, O_2, and N_2, which seem at a glance to be so similar, are in fact very different—one is a stable gas, one is a flammable gas, and one is a highly explosive gas. I then asked them to explain why that was the case. I thought this was a clever question to ask my students for two reasons. For one, these three molecules had the three different kinds of covalent bonds we had talked about (single, double, and triple), so the students would have to analyze and represent all three kinds. And for another, the students would get to discover for themselves an answer to the question about why it's important to understand structures of molecules; they would see for themselves the correlation between structures and properties of molecules, a very important chemistry framework.

I passed out the question in class. I waited for them to draw the three molecules. I waited for them to have the "aha" moment when they would realize that the most stable one had a triple bond, the flammable one had the double bond, and the highly explosive one just had a single bond. I waited for them to be impressed that the pictures they scribbled on paper to analyze the bonding actually helped them predict the way those gases behave in the real world. But none of that happened. Much to my shock, not a single student (in a class full of students who had become really good at drawing structures of molecules) drew a structure of H_2, O_2, or N_2. I was looking over their shoulders at papers containing wild explanations about unrelated gas, air, and water concepts. Where were their pictures? Where was their analysis of the bonds and the structures of these three molecules?

I suggested they turn their papers over and start again by figuring out how to draw the three molecules first and then answering the question. They were very annoyed with me because I hadn't told them to draw the pictures to begin with. "How were we supposed to know that we needed to draw the structures if the question didn't ask us to do that?" In reflecting on that experience after class, I realized that in nine years of studying chemistry at the undergraduate and graduate level, I had learned to think like a chemist in a way that had become as normal and automatic and subconscious to me as speaking Setswana was to Kagiso.

With my experience in class that day came the realization that, while I do think like a chemist, I wasn't really aware of what that meant. I realized that to teach chemistry effectively I would have to make clear to my students these ways of thinking that I myself had internalized and was no longer really aware of doing—just as I had had to do when I taught English as a second language in Botswana. Since then I have been able to identify some of my ways of thinking that are distinctly due to my chemistry background; many of my discoveries came from noticing where students and I differed in our approaches.

In this chapter, I address six of the cognitive processes or ways of thinking I have discovered:

- Considering structure to explain properties
- Seeking patterns
- Using models
- Developing a specialized vocabulary
- Understanding that numbers are relative to a context
- Connecting abstractions with real-world experiences

I will first explain how chemists use each of these cognitive processes and how/why beginning students fail to use them. Then I will explain how I deliberately teach my students to think in these ways. I will describe some of the pedagogical approaches I use in my classes, and I will provide examples of performance assessments I use to follow and evaluate my students' progress. Since I believe that learning how to think like a chemist is a developmental process, I will provide examples that show how my students are expected to use these cognitive processes in increasingly sophisticated and independent ways. In some sections I will show this development by providing examples from the beginning and end of a freshman chemistry course I teach. In other sections I provide examples from both my freshman level chemistry course and my junior level biochemistry course. It is my hope that as you read the chapter you will see the relevance of these ways of thinking to your own discipline or that you might gain insight into some of your discipline's unique ways of thinking. I hope that you find some of my strategies for teaching these cognitive processes helpful in your own courses.

Chemists Consider Structure

The scenario described in the introduction, in which freshman students were to explain why the properties of H_2, O_2, and N_2 varied significantly, was one in which I realized my students differed from me in their approach to a chemical problem. Chemists pretty automatically start discussions about a chemical with some explanation of the chemical's structure. In my field of biochemistry, for example, every presentation on an enzyme starts with pictures and explanations of that enzyme's structure. Every journal article on a protein includes in the background section a reference to the research done on the structure of the protein. Once the structure of a chemical is known, properties and functions can be inferred (and then verified with experimentation). This is why I had assumed my students in the freshman chemistry example above would also automatically explore the structure of H_2, O_2, and N_2 in order to explain why one was stable, one was flammable, and one was highly explosive. When students learn to think like chemists, they know how to approach that question; without being told, they would first figure out the structures of those molecules.

Teaching Students to Consider Structure

As the example above illustrates, students will not automatically apply the structure-property or structure-function frameworks when given a problem that requires that kind of analysis. I still use the pop quiz described above. But now I tell the students that, after they give the problem an honest effort, they can come to me for direction. My first suggestion would be, "Use the structure-property framework." If they ask for further direction, I would say, "To use the structure-property framework, first draw the Lewis Structures of the three molecules, then infer properties based on the Lewis Structures." I intentionally give the suggestions out one at a time because I want to respond directly to students' questions. I want my students to wonder before the first suggestion, "How can I possibly know anything about the properties of these molecules?" And I want them to wonder before the second suggestion, "What is a structure-property framework?"

Initially they need to be told to use the framework. During other class activities they may need to be reminded. Eventually they should be applying the framework on their own. Figure 6.1 is a question that I ask on one of the first assessments in that freshman course. The question reminds the students to consider structure in order to infer some properties. The question is also designed so that students cannot rely on memorized information but must really analyze the molecules.

In a later assessment in that same freshman course, students are asked a question that again requires a structural analysis in order to make some infer-

---

Last night a large meteorite hit Alverno's campus right outside the Campus Center. As a class project the CH 113 students decide to examine the meteorite and evaluate its composition. To your surprise you discover a new element with a mass of 285, an atomic number of 117, and an electron configuration of $[RN]5f^{14}6d^{10}7s^2p^5$. You estimate that its electronegativity is about 2.0. In honor of the site on which this new element was first discovered you decide to name it Alvernium.

- *Use a diagram to show where on the periodic table this new element belongs.*

- *What ionic charge would you expect it to form, and why?*

- *You were able to form two new compounds from Alvernium which have the molecular formulas CAv_4 and $AvCl$. Would you expect these compounds to be polar or nonpolar? Explain your answer using Lewis Structures.*

- *You next try to determine the solubility of your two new compounds. Would you expect either of your new compounds to dissolve in water? Explain your answer using some type of a figure.*

FIGURE 6.1

EARLY ASSESSMENT IN FRESHMAN CHEMISTRY[1]

Directing Students to Use the Structure-Property Framework

ences about properties and functions (figure 6.2). This time they do not receive any prompt to consider the structure. Most students are doing so automatically by this point.

In the first assessment question, I remind the students to first draw the Lewis Structures before analyzing the properties (polarity and solubility). In the second assessment question I ask the students a question that can be answered only if the structures of the steroid and the glucuronate ester of 11-β-HEC are considered. This time, however, I don't tell the students to think about the structures first; at this point in the course, the students know to do this—they are beginning to think like chemists. As they move into other courses, students are expected to analyze increasingly more complicated structures. Repeated exposure to this framework in multiple contexts helps students to internalize this cognitive process.

Chemists Look for Patterns

A common student response (or lack thereof) that really surprised me in my first year of teaching chemistry occurred in the lab. The first time I saw it, a student was collecting data on a spectrophotometer from a set of samples that she had prepared. I was beside her watching as she measured each test tube. I was impressed with her data; each test tube absorbed twice as much light as the one before it. I commented after each test tube, "Wow! Look at that! Great data!" The student, on the other hand, was not impressed at all. "Are these right?" was her only question.

Steroidal hormones are members of the lipid class. Steroidal hormones that are no longer needed and are not toxic must be excreted. But they are not directly excreted in the urine. They are converted in the liver to the glucuronate ester of 11-β-HEC, which is then sent out via the urine. The reaction is shown on the front of the assessment. If the body is efficient, does it make sense to take these extra (and energy consuming) steps to get rid of waste steroids? Why?

FIGURE 6.2
LATER ASSESSMENT IN FRESHMAN CHEMISTRY
Eliciting Independent Use of the Structure-Property Framework

I realized that I was thinking like a chemist, and she was not. Chemists get excited (or relieved) by patterns and trends in their data. I will never forget the time in my first year of graduate school when I was part of a team of people gathered around a computer with the DNA sequence that we had just determined after months of experiments. We were "playing with it" in an attempt to find some pattern in all that data. We were left breathless with excitement when we finally noticed that the 2,500 base pairs could be aligned into ~70 repeats of a 35 base pair motif. When we see a pattern like that, we don't ask, "Is it right?" Instead, we ask, "What does it mean?" Often we use mathematics frameworks to analyze the pattern (is it linear? direct? indirect? logarithmic?) and then draw chemical inferences from these patterns. The 35 base pair motif that I found in graduate school was just the right size to interact with the protein actin; this data was consistent with our hypothesis about the function of our protein as a scaffold for actin.

The opposite of patterns/trends is chaos and randomness. That's frustrating to us. Was there a mistake in our design of the experiment? Was there a mistake in the way we conducted the experiment? Is there really no relationship between the variables we're testing? Many of our experimental results look like this, with no apparent pattern in the data. Then we repeat the experiments, hoping to catch our mistake, or we modify the experiments, or we move our research in a different direction until we once again discover patterns in our data.

First-year students watch without interest as the numbers appear one at a time on the spectrophotometer. When students learn to think like chemists, though, they will quickly sketch graphs of their data on scratch paper as they measure each test tube, because they can't wait to see what their results look like. And in the event that their data turns out linear, they will be thrilled. They will never ask, "Is this right?"

Teaching Students to Look for Patterns

Since I want my students to look for patterns in their data, I've learned to refrain from saying, "Wow! Look at that! Great data!" as I look over their shoulders when they're doing their experiments. Instead I will stop them as they are collecting data and ask them what they think of the data so far. If they tell me that it "looks good," I will ask them why they think so. To make sure they understand the pattern that is unfolding, I will ask them, as they are working, to predict the next data point.

One of the most important strategies I've used for helping students understand the significance of patterns in data is the assignment of independent lab projects in which students determine the two variables they will compare and plan how to test them; ironically, one of the reasons that independent projects serve as powerful learning experiences is because they so often lead to results that don't fall into a pattern. If students always do "cookbook" prepackaged experiments that are set up for them, they won't appreciate that most experimental results do not fall into nice patterns, at least not on the first try. In fact, students often have the false impression that any two variables tested in the lab are related somehow. Students need to have disappointing random results a few times to understand and appreciate the significance of data that follows a trend. For this reason, I have students designing their own experiments beginning in their first year. Many times the two variables they choose to study do not have a nice clear relationship, or the experiment they conduct is not appropriate for showing the relationship. These always turn out to be important learning experiences.

One independent lab assessment that my freshman students take is described in figure 6.3. In the second part of the lab assessment, students determine how the height to which the water rises in the glass is affected by some variable that they think up. In many cases, they do not get nice linear data; sometimes it is difficult to tell in their data if there's a relationship at all, and sometimes there clearly is no relationship.

The first time I used the experiment described in figure 6.3, I was surprised by the reaction of the students who found no pattern in their data at all. They thought for sure that they had done something wrong in conducting the experiment. They did not consider at all that there would be no relationship between, say, the initial height of the water in the pan and the height to which the water would rise in the glass. Their reaction is not so surprising, because until then they had probably always done experiments in which their teachers had set up two related variables for testing.

While freshmen are exposed to simple patterns in their data and learn how to graph data and make predictions from their graphs, juniors are asked to think about their data more deeply. I have found that it is especially important to allow students plenty of time to discuss their data in groups to help them develop this ability to recognize and interpret patterns. In an

You almost certainly know that if you put a glass over a burning candle, the candle will soon go out. But you have probably never gathered data about this process or looked for patterns or trends in the data. In this assessment you will design experiments to look for trends. Before you begin, get used to the system you will be working with by following these directions:

1. Place a mound of clay on the bottom of a dissecting pan (a metal pan with wax on the bottom) and add water to a depth of 1 to 2 cm.
2. Place a candle in the center of the mound of clay and light it.
3. Quickly place a glass over the candle so the rim of the glass is under water. Repeat this experiment three or four times. Observe carefully. Write your observations down.
4. Put a rubber band around the glass. Repeat the experiment using the rubber band to mark the final height of water in the glass after the candle goes out and the water rises.
5. Measure the final height of the water in the glass. Record the height.

Experiment #1
HYPOTHESIS: You will be repeating the procedure you just did with an increasing number of candles to test a hypothesis. Write down your hypothesis.

DATA: You have already collected one data point for testing your hypothesis. You will conduct an experiment in which you test two, three, five, and six candles. Create a data table to record the results of your experiment.

DATA ANALYSIS: Graph the final height of the water versus the number of candles.

CONCLUSIONS: Write a conclusion based on your graph.

Experiment #2
Other factors or variables might be related to the final height of the water in the glass. Choose one of these factors (or think of another one): initial depth of water in the pan, size of glass, type of rubber band, height of candle, etc. Develop a hypothesis about how the factor you selected is related to the final height of the water, design and conduct an experiment to test your hypothesis, record your results in a data table, graph your data, and write a conclusion based on your graph.

Criteria for Assessment:
1. Correctly uses important terms related to doing science
2. Makes accurate, complete observations
3. Uses observations to make reasonable inferences
4. Distinguishes between observations and inferences
5. Identifies patterns and regularities in both numerical and qualitative observations
6. Develops and tests hypotheses
7. Uses metric units correctly
8. Graphs numerical data appropriately
9. Uses graphs to make reasonable predictions
10. Keeps a complete written record of her work (observations, inferences, hypotheses, testing procedure, graph, predictions)

FIGURE 6.3
LAB ASSESSMENT IN FRESHMAN CHEMISTRY[2]
Searching for Data Patterns

assessment in my junior level biochemistry course, students receive a set of discussion questions that prompt them to further analyze and evaluate the data they have collected in their laboratory notebooks. The group assessment is set up to give students an experience similar to the weekly lab meetings that are commonplace among researchers. Students share and compare their data in groups in order to answer the questions posed. Figure 6.4 is a transcript from a videotaped discussion of one group of my junior biochemistry students. They are trying to figure out why their absorbance data did not double in one set of experiments. In their conversation, the students think more deeply about the patterns in their data than they had in their original analysis in their notebooks.

Students' understanding of the importance of patterns in data becomes more sophisticated as they progress through the chemistry curriculum. The assessment question in figure 6.4 challenges these students to think more deeply about a pattern (linear) with which they are already very familiar. Students also develop the ability to analyze increasingly more complicated patterns (from linear to logarithmic, for example) in their data sets. They are thinking like chemists when they can provide a rationale for why they think two variables will be related, when they can set up an experiment with the proper controls to determine a relationship between two (or more) variables, and when they can use models and quantitative analysis to make sense of the patterns that emerge in their data.

Chemists Use Models

The molecules we study are too small to see. The reactions and processes we study are too fast to see. So chemists use models or mental images. Models are meant to be tools. I came to the realization in my first years of teaching chemistry that my students had to learn how to use these tools. In one of my freshman chemistry courses, I teach students a model of the atom called the Bohr model. Every semester I teach students how to draw Bohr models of atoms and how to use those models to predict bonding. One time a student came up to me and said that her boyfriend at a large university was using the orbital model, not the Bohr model. She wanted to know which one was right. (And by her tone I think her real question was "Why are we learning an incorrect model of the atom?") I didn't understand at the time that this student was really asking, "What does an atom look like—the Bohr model I

Assessment Question:

In experiment 2, when you doubled the amount of Coomassie Blue, your absorbance should have doubled. Did the absorbance double when you doubled the amount of pNP in experiment 3? Why or why not? Did the absorbance double when you doubled the amount of BSA in experiment 8? Why or why not?

TRANSCRIPT OF STUDENT DISCUSSION:

"My absorbances were .15 and .275, so it's a little less than double. Is that what yours were?"

"Mine is a little more than doubled."

"So it isn't doubled."

"I don't know . . . Mine really didn't double."

"Okay, so why didn't they double then?"

"Yeah mine didn't either. It wasn't as obvious as the others at least. Why didn't they double there?"

"Maybe it's because we added the biuret reagent and you had to subtract that from your data."

"So it wasn't just reading the absorbance of BSA, it was reading the absorbance of BSA minus the [biuret reagent]"

"But if you're looking at both actual absorbances with it minus [the biuret reagent]..."

"Both of them have it subtracted out."

"Okay"

"I think it really should double."

"I think it should too. But was your graph linear?"

"Mine was linear. You know what, what was our slope on the other graphs?" Maybe the slope has something to do with it.

"It does. It can still be linear and not double. You know what I mean. Not every line that you follow goes up one and over one."

"My concentration and absorbance curve of BSA was really good. I got an R^2 of .999. So that's about as good as you can get – and it didn't double."

FIGURE 6.4

GROUP ASSESSMENT IN BIOCHEMISTRY

Collaborative Work to Recognize and Interpret Patterns

draw or the orbital model he draws?" The answer to the question she asked is, "Both are correct." One correctly represents the energy levels of electrons in an atom and one correctly represents the statistical probability of finding an electron at a certain location relative to the nucleus. However, the answer to the real question she meant is "neither." Neither model is in any way an "image" of an atom.

I've come to realize that students take models as literal images. In fact, they confuse textbook schematics with textbook microscopy images. If they consider models as these sorts of literal images, they won't understand the uses or limitations of each model, and they won't understand the need to bounce back and forth between models, sometimes using more than one.

Teaching Students to Use Models

Three of Alverno's chemistry outcomes are related to models in chemistry. They include the ability to

- Communicate effectively, using the language, concepts, and models of chemistry
- Use different strategies and models of chemistry to analyze and synthesize chemical data
- Critique the data, strategies, and models of chemistry[3]

Students first need to learn what chemists mean by models. In my introductory chemistry course for freshmen, I show a videotape called *Modeling the Unseen*.[4] The video provides a variety of examples of models, such as a model for IO (a moon of Jupiter), the kinetic particle model of gases, and the lock-and-key model of enzyme-inhibiting drug compounds. Students answer four questions as they watch the video: What is a model? How do scientists make or develop models? What examples of models are discussed in the videotape? What are models generally used for?

My very favorite part of the video is a short segment that takes place in an elementary school classroom with a visiting scientist teaching the children about models. He has two locked black briefcases. He wants the children to develop a mental image of what is inside the briefcases. After shaking the briefcases as hard as they can, the children conclude that one briefcase has metal in it and the other briefcase has either nothing in it or something very light. The children suggest that an X-ray would be helpful for developing their model. The scientist does have X-rays for each. In one X-ray, you can see nails. In the other X-ray, nothing shows up. Then the children are very convinced that one suitcase has nails and the other one is empty. When the scientist opens up the suitcase with nails, the kids clap; they are pleased that the contents of the briefcase match their mental image. When the scientist opens up the "empty" briefcase, cotton balls fall out all over the place; the children gasp in disbelief. It is an impressive illustration for my students of a key limitation of models: They are only as accurate as the data from which they are derived.

The videotape described above is just an introduction to models used in my freshman chemistry course. Throughout subsequent chemistry courses, chemistry faculty continue to emphasize how and why models are used. One of the goals of my junior level biochemistry course is for students to understand the structural information provided in a variety of two-dimensional (2-D) representations of the four main classes of biomolecules. At the end of the semester I assess their understanding of the 2-D representations as models of three-dimensional (3-D) biomolecules. The assessment is described in figure 6.5. In the assessment, I meet with students in groups of three and give each of them two figures of biomolecules as stimuli for our discussion. I have them explain what the figures show and what they fail to show about the structure of the biomolecules. I want them to recognize that a biomolecule can be accurately represented in a variety of ways. Each model is intended to provide different structural information.

I have found this assessment to be a very valuable way for me to diagnose and correct any misconceptions the students in my junior level biochemistry course may have regarding the many different ways of representing biomolecules on paper. For example, there are computer images of biomolecules "opened up" to help illustrate localized folding. Because students take models literally, they often think that those images represent the molecules in an early folding stage; they don't understand, at first, that the images are artificial in the sense that the biomolecules never really look opened up like that.

In other assignments, I help students better understand 2-D representations of molecules by having them transform 2-D images on paper into 3-D models using a variety of model kits.[5] Working with 3-D models helps students better understand the limitations of the 2-D images used all the time in textbooks, journal articles, computer programs, and scientific presentations.

ASSESSMENT DIRECTIONS:

You will be assigned to a group of three and to a 45-minute time block for your oral assessment on the biomolecules. During the assessment I will randomly give each of you two images to discuss (DNA, protein, mRNA, tRNA, rRNA, carbohydrates, or lipids). The images will be from some source other than your textbook. You should come prepared to address the following for the biomolecules you receive:

1. *Identify the biomolecule in the figure as specifically as possible.*

2. *Explain what the figure shows about the structure of the biomolecule. (Use the biochemistry structure framework.)*

3. *Explain what the figure fails to show about the structure of the biomolecule.*

4. *Explain what the function of that biomolecule is as specifically as you can.*

5. *Explain the synthesis of the biomolecule in vivo.*

FIGURE 6.5

ORAL ASSESSMENT IN BIOCHEMISTRY

Analyzing the Structure of Biomolecules from 2-D Representations

Equations are another kind of model that chemists use. Equations help chemists organize and communicate data. Students in my junior level biochemistry course use some kinetic models for analyzing enzyme data. They write up formal reports for these studies in which they synthesize and analyze data from several experiments. Before they turn in the formal lab reports, I have them do a preliminary assignment in which they answer questions about the models they use in their data analysis. The questions are provided in figure 6.6.

The assignment in figure 6.6 is meant to reinforce the idea that students are using models (equations, in this case) as an organizing principle by which they can make some sense of their data and as a vehicle for communicating their experimental results. With these preliminary guide questions, students are more deliberate in using models in their lab reports.

With repeated exposure to a variety of models in all their chemistry

1. *List all graphs by title that you will include in your report in the order they will appear. Make sure that the order is logical, the list is complete, and no two graphs really show the exact same thing.*

2. *List the biochemistry models you used for each graph along with a reference that describes that model.*

3. *Provide each graph (fully labeled) and give a one-sentence conclusion for each of your graphs. You may use any program you wish for graphing your data. Show all calculations you used prior to graphing your data, and show all calculations relevant to analyzing your graph.*

4. *List all of your graphs that indicate your data is unreliable and briefly explain why you think so (i.e., the data should be hyperbolic according to the Michaelis-Menton model, but it is scattered instead). Make sure that you offer some explanations in your report as to why this data did not turn out as expected.*

FIGURE 6.6

DATA ANALYSIS ASSIGNMENT IN BIOCHEMISTRY

Reflecting on Use of Models for Analyzing Data

courses, students become increasingly competent at using models. At first they just learn what models are. Then they start using them and thinking about the data from which the models were derived. At a more sophisticated level they understand the assumptions and limitations of models. And finally in senior level courses they begin critiquing models.

Chemists Use Specialized Vocabulary

Unfortunately for students, chemists use a lot of words (such as *entropy* and *valence electrons* and *ionic bonds*) that are not a part of everyday vocabulary and that are not used in any other context. Also, many terms used in chemistry have quite a different meaning in non-chemistry contexts. For example, gas that you put in your car is really a liquid and not a gas at all to a chemist. Boiling a potato is not really boiling it at all to a chemist because the potato has not vaporized but is still a solid. An empty bottle is not really empty to a chemist but contains bouncing gas molecules. The same thing occurs in other disciplines; physicists, for example, say that a car that is slowing down is experiencing "acceleration."

Like learning any other language, memorizing definitions does not work; that's not how I developed my chemical vocabulary. (And I certainly couldn't learn to communicate in Setswana just by studying the Setswana/English dictionary.) Consider my understanding of the term "clone." If I had learned about clones using the glossary of a textbook, I would understand that a clone is a large number of cells identical to a single ancestral cell. (I looked that up to write this paragraph.) Instead, I learned about clones the first time I used one. I will never forget going to the $-70°C$ freezer to pull out my clone; my lab mates kept an eye on me from their lab benches to make sure I got in and out of the freezer quickly so their clones wouldn't thaw. I will also never forget waking up in a panic in the middle of the night unsure if I had remembered to store in that $-70°C$ freezer a portion of the clone I had "grown up" for my experiments. If I had not properly set aside a small sample, that clone was lost forever. There was no one else using it, no place to buy it, no way to "remake" it, but if I had set aside a small portion in the $-70°C$ freezer, that clone could be used again and again and again, forever. My experience with a clone provided me with a far richer (and more useful) understanding of that term than a dictionary definition ever could.

A student quizzed me once. She had just purchased something like a "Dictionary of Biochemical Terms." (I'm sure part of the reason that she pulled it out to quiz me was that she wanted me to be impressed that she had bought such a book.) She randomly flipped to a page, rolled her finger down the text, and asked me to define a "zinc finger." When I told her it was a structural motif in a protein, one that interacts with DNA, she was sure I had a photographic memory. The truth is I did not have that definition memorized. I had done sequence analysis in graduate school, and I used a program that automatically searched for some common motifs. The printout that I always got from the analysis had the motifs grouped together. The zinc finger was always grouped with the leucine zipper, and I had read about the leucine zipper in a paper I presented for a journal club. So I accessed in my mind a series of experiences I had and connections I had made in order to come up with a definition for the zinc finger fairly easily. My years of research provided me with many such experiences and connections that would have helped me to create a definition for most of the terms in her book.

Teaching Students a Specialized Vocabulary

One of Alverno's chemistry outcomes emphasizes the importance of using specialized vocabulary. It is the ability to "communicate effectively, using the language, concepts, and models of chemistry." In nearly every assessment I give, there is at least one criterion related to this outcome. One of the criteria from a written assessment I give is to "use vocabulary correctly in describing polarity, intermolecular forces, physical properties, and physical states." One of the criteria for a speech I assign is to "use technical terminology accurately and appropriately."

I have used several pedagogical strategies to help students develop the specialized vocabulary that chemists use. Having students copy definitions from the book and write them down on an assessment has been the least effective, and I no longer do that. The strategies I do use include

- Providing students with experiences to work with the terms
- Having students construct their own definitions
- Having students relate chemistry terms to their own non-chemistry vocabulary
- Having students map relationships between terms
- Providing students with authentic contexts for using the terms

The first of these strategies is to provide students with experiences they can connect to the terms. For example, rather than having them memorize that isomers are substances that have the same number and kind of atoms arranged differently, I have them work in groups to draw on newsprint as many different kinds of structures as they can with the formula $C_4H_{10}O$. They always incorrectly draw a few that look different on paper but are actually identical in 3-D space. I have them use their model kits and put those together. They begin to recognize that some of their structures are identical and some are "isomers" (but they don't have a word for that yet). When the group gets all possibilities drawn and eliminates all identical structures, I say, "Great—what you've got on your newsprint now are isomers of $C_4H_{10}O$."

That term has meaning for my students because of the work they did together.

The second strategy I use is to help students construct their own definitions. In the freshman chemistry course that I teach, on the very first day of class I have them work in groups to create two lists: one of "stuff" that is matter and one of "stuff" that is not. Inevitably they wonder about air (because it's invisible), gas (which they don't relate to air), energy (because it has no mass), and light and sound (which they don't recognize as kinds of energy). I help them categorize all these based on questions they raise. I also prompt them to think about other things like fear and friendship and history. (Then I'm sorry I did because they start asking about flames and magnetism and souls.) When I'm convinced they can classify things as matter or nonmatter, I have them jot down in their own words a definition of matter.

A third strategy I use is to help students relate chemistry terms to their non-chemistry use of the same or similar terms. Before we talk about ionic and covalent bonds, for example, I ask them what they mean (outside of chemistry) when they talk about a "bond." "Things sticking together" actually works for both male bonding and ionic bonding. I also use this strategy when I teach students how to classify matter. The definitions for pure compounds, pure elements, homogeneous mixtures, and heterogeneous mixtures are difficult ones for students to grasp. Before I even give them those technical classifications of matter, I have the students do the following: define *pure* in your own words, define *mixture* in your own words, list some pure things you know about, list some mixtures you know about, list some things you know about that look pure but are really mixtures. This set of questions always results in students asking great questions to lead into the technical terms—questions like, "Is water a mixture since it is made up of hydrogen and oxygen? Is the oxygen administered in hospitals pure? What about white wine? Are all natural things pure?"

A fourth strategy I use is to have students map the relationship between terms. Much has been written on concept mapping. One article, "Teaching Students to Construct Graphic Representations," explains the benefits of having students represent text in graphic outlines.[6] The article also provides generic models and guidelines for constructing graphic representations, and offers suggestions for teaching students to create helpful concept maps. I have found concept mapping very valuable for helping students discover the relationships between new terms they are learning.

Finally, I use authentic contexts to motivate students to learn vocabulary. I learned how powerful context can be for developing vocabulary when I taught a junior level organic chemistry course for one of our faculty members on sabbatical leave. This is a course where students traditionally learn a very complicated set of International Union of Pure and Applied Chemistry (IUPAC) rules for naming organic chemicals. In organic courses everywhere, students learn more and more of these rules as the course progresses and take tests where they name organic compounds or draw them if given the name. I was surprised, then, when I looked at my colleague's syllabus and did not see any objectives related to this. As I progressed through teaching my colleague's course, I learned why I didn't need to stress this topic. One of the first lab projects that the students did was an independent project in which they had to use chemical catalogues to order their own starting materials. Chemical catalogues are thousands of pages long with long lists of chemicals on each page, and all chemicals are listed by their proper IUPAC name. Students found that they were unable to locate their chemicals in these catalogues if their protocols used the common names instead of the IUPAC names. They practically begged me to teach them about naming organic chemicals. In this case, context was a strong motivator. Other authentic contexts I use in my courses include panel presentations, speeches, group discussions, and interviews; all of these require the students to use chemical terms in communicating their information and ideas.

Chemists Have a Sense of Numbers Being Relative to a Context

If you tell chemists that a pill provides 100 μg of some mineral, we need to know how many micrograms one needs in a daily diet because the quantity 100 μg by itself does not impress us as large or small. If you ask us what 100 plus 100 is, we will ask 100 of what plus 100 of what, because, for example, 100 mL of water plus 100 mL of sugar will not make up 200 mL of sugar water. If you tell us that your results were off by only 100 nanomoles, we would ask you what your percent error was before we would congratulate you on your accuracy.

I have learned that students see numbers differently than I do. A student in a freshman course I taught wanted to determine if broccoli loses vitamin C when it is boiled. She boiled some broccoli at home, brought it in to the lab, completed a titration experiment, did some calculations, and ended up with a number. She had accurately determined the amount of vitamin C in her sample and showed me her results. "Does this number seem right to you?" she asked. Although she did not see any meaning at all in that number, she thought I would because she was sure that a number had to have some meaning. In fact, it didn't have much meaning to me either. I needed to see that number relative to an unboiled control. Or I needed to compare her results to some published information on vitamin C in raw broccoli, but then I would need to know how the size of her sample compared to the sample used in the published data. When students learn to think like chemists, they learn that before they ever even conduct an experiment they need to plan how they will make meaning out of quantitative results.

Teaching Students to Understand That Numbers Are Relative

In assignments, lab reports, and assessments, I always include prompt questions that get students to think more deeply about their numerical answers. For example, in the preliminary lab to the titration experiment described above, students determined the amount of vitamin C in a juice sample and in a piece of fruit. To help them make meaning out of their numerical answers, they were asked to address three questions in their lab report:

- A typical serving of juice is 1 cup or 240 mL. How many milligrams of vitamin C are in one serving of the juice that you titrated?
- How many grams of the fruit or vegetable used in this lab contain the recommended daily allowance (60 milligrams of vitamin C)?
- How many servings of juice or pieces of fruit would you need to eat to get the recommended daily allowance of vitamin C?

These questions help them rethink their conclusions relative to a typical serving and relative to a recommended daily allowance.

Rarely do I have students just do a calculation and report an answer. In my freshman chemistry course I almost always prompt them to provide a meaning for their numerical answer. Figure 6.7 contains an assessment question from a unit in which my students do solution and dilution calculations. I set an authentic context for the question, which makes it more reasonable for the students to go beyond just doing the calculation.

As a lab assistant, you are given the following directions. Explain exactly how you would prepare the following solutions.

1. *Prepare 500 mL of a 0.15 M NaCl (F.W. = 58).*

   Calculation:

   Explanation:

2. *How would you dilute the above 0.15 M NaCl solution to prepare 50 mL of a .01 M solution?*

   Calculation:

   Explanation:

FIGURE 6.7

ASSESSMENT IN FRESHMAN CHEMISTRY

Explaining the Meaning of Calculated Values

Likewise, students in my junior level biochemistry course need to write about the meaning of their numerical conclusions in their lab notebooks. There are three criteria by which I evaluate their conclusions:

- You address the objectives stated in the introduction.
- You clearly interpret the results obtained.
- You discuss the expected results and why they were or were not achieved.

In a written assessment that follows their lab notebook work, I ask my students to do calculations similar to ones they've done in their lab work. I again ask questions that will encourage students to make meaning out of their numerical data. Figure 6.8 contains questions from that junior level assessment.

Initially, students need prompt questions like the ones in figures 6.7 and 6.8, or they consider their work done once they get a number on the calcula-

1. *NaF is a very strong inhibitor, and you may need to dilute your solution. How could you prepare 500 mL of 1.2 mM NaF by diluting the 6 mM NaF solution? Does your answer make sense? Why?*

2. *In experiment 3 you determined the extinction coefficient of uracil in water at 260 nm by measuring the absorption of a 50 μM uracil solution in a 1 cm quartz cuvette. Most of you came very close to the correct value, which is 8.2 cm^{-1} mM^{-1}. What is the absorbance you should have found for your 50 μM solution to give you the correct extinction coefficient?*

3. *In experiment 6 you were supposed to mix 20 mL of a 20 mM K_2HPO_4 solution with 10 mL of a 20 mM KH_2PO_4 solution to prepare a 20 mM phosphate buffer with a pH of 7.2. One student accidentally used 10 mL of the K_2HPO_4 solution and 20 mL of the KH_2PO_4 solution (she got them backwards). What was the pH of her buffer? Does your answer make sense? Why? Note: The pKa for a phosphate buffer is 6.9.*

4. *If you measured the pH of the above buffer and you found it to be 7.1 instead of 7.2, what is your percent error?*

FIGURE 6.8

ASSESSMENT IN BIOCHEMISTRY

Reflecting on the Meaning of Calculated Values

tor. With repeated exposure to these prompt questions in multiple settings, however, students internalize the habit of asking, "Does this number make sense? To what can I compare it in order to extract some meaning?" When they are thinking like chemists, they no longer need the prompt questions to remind them to make meaning of their quantitative data.

Chemists Connect Abstractions with Real-World Experiences

Chemists study the "real world," but we do so at an abstract level. While molecules can be seen when they are stuck together in large groups (as when 602,000,000,000,000,000,000,000 water molecules are stuck together in a coffee cup), chemists study individual molecules that are too small to see.

Also, chemists study the changes those molecules undergo; we study the steps in those changes (which happen too fast to see), and we also study the invisible forces which drive those changes. The concepts surrounding change are the most difficult ones for students to grasp. The explanations are quantitative, with formulas and constants. Once the students start doing the math, however, they seem to completely lose the connection between these chemical concepts and their own physical reality, as illustrated in the following example.

In one set of exercises in freshman chemistry, I teach students how to do a thermodynamic analysis of change, and they use the formula $\Delta G = \Delta H - T\Delta S$ to determine whether or not processes can occur. When they seem fairly comfortable with the meaning of the three variables (ΔG, ΔH, and ΔS), I give them a question that they can solve only if they consider the relationships between the three variables. I hand out a problem with a picture of a half-frozen lake. Then I ask them to determine which is more likely—will the lake completely melt or completely freeze? Working in groups, the students start in on their thermodynamic analysis. Usually about one-third of my students will conclude that it will freeze, one-third will conclude that it will melt, and one-third will say they don't know how to figure it out. Why are my students unable to answer this question? (*You* can answer it, right?) One semester a student asked me a question that has clarified my students' thinking for me. She wanted to know, "Are you asking if it would melt or freeze in the real world or according to thermodynamic analysis?" These students were completely willing to say that it would most likely freeze (despite their own experience that a half-frozen lake melts in the spring) or that it would most likely melt (even though they've seen half-frozen lakes completely freeze over) if their thermodynamic analysis led them to that answer.

As a chemist, I use frameworks that are consistent with the real world. If I were given the above question, I would say (as you probably did), "In my experience, the half-frozen lake can go either way—it depends on the temperature." Then I would analyze the equation to see if it shows the same result as my experience (and it does!). If they're not consistent, I question the equation or my use of the equation. I do not question my experience with melting and freezing lakes. When my student asked, "Are you asking if it would melt or freeze in the real world or according to thermodynamic analysis," she saw a real dichotomy between theory and her own experiences.

Teaching Students to Connect Abstractions with Real-World Experiences

Students need help moving between abstract ideas and real-world experiences. For example, they need help moving between the microscopic world of individual molecules and the macroscopic world of connected molecules. In my freshman course when they are looking at intermolecular forces (such as the hydrogen bonds that hold water together), I have them predict how many drops of water will fit on a penny; they are always amazed at how "sticky" water is as they pile up drop after drop on the penny before it spills over. Those sticky water droplets are a manifestation at the macroscopic level of trillions and trillions of hydrogen bonds at the microscopic level. Likewise, when we talk about melting points of ionic compounds versus covalent compounds, I have them imagine melting salt in one frying pan and sugar in another and think about which melts most easily; I am helping them to connect theory (about the relationship between intermolecular forces and physical properties) with their own experiences in the world.

Another area in which students need help moving from abstractions to real world is when they are using equations (such as the Gibb's free energy equation described above). I like to have students think about the meaning of the variables in equations before I have them do any calculations. For example, before I teach my freshman chemistry students how to use a formula for calculating concentrations of diluted solutions ($V_1C_1 = V_2C_2$), I give them the exercise described in figure 6.9.

Students also need help with abstractions when it comes to chemistry concepts surrounding change. It does not help that most examples and practice problems given in textbooks involve changes in test tubes (because many real-world changes are too complex for students to analyze in a freshman chemistry course). One exercise I use to address this dilemma is to simply ask my freshman students which change framework, kinetic or thermodynamic, could be used to analyze the changes given in figure 6.10. They do not know enough about either of those frameworks to actually answer the questions, but I want them to know that chemistry frameworks can be used

1. *Put one teaspoon of sugar in a cup of coffee. Put one teaspoon of sugar in a pot of coffee. Which one will taste sweeter (i.e., in which one is the sugar more concentrated)?*

2. *Pour some coffee from the pot in the above question into a second coffee cup. In which is the sugar more concentrated now (the coffee pot or the second coffee cup)?*

3. *Compare the three coffees above: the first cup, the coffee pot, and the second cup. In which one is the amount of sugar the greatest? In which one is the amount of sugar the least? In which one is the concentration of sugar the greatest? In which one is the concentration of sugar the least?*

4. *In your own words, describe "concentration."*

FIGURE 6.9
DISCUSSION QUESTIONS IN FRESHMAN CHEMISTRY
Thinking about the Meaning of Variables in a Formula

to address real-world phenomena. The frameworks are not reserved for test tubes.

Freshmen need these kinds of questions because they don't understand that the abstract ideas they are learning in chemistry are ways of understanding and explaining the real world. The student who wanted to know, "Are you asking if it would melt or freeze in the real world or according to thermodynamic analysis?" was not unique in her thinking. With repeated examples connecting abstract ideas to their own experiences, students begin to make the connections on their own. Eventually it is the students, not I, who make the connections between the freezing point of depression and throwing salt on a frozen sidewalk, between competitive inhibition of an enzyme's active site and AZT treatment in AIDS, between the lactic acid production in anaerobic respiration and achy muscles after a tough workout. It's not uncommon for my juniors in biochemistry to ask, "Does that have anything to do with . . . ?" as they try to connect a biochemistry concept to something they've seen or heard about in their own experiences. I love those questions. To me they show that my students are thinking like chemists.

Which chemistry framework would you use to answer these questions?

1. *I'm wondering if I can take allergy medicine tonight given that I will be nursing my baby tomorrow morning. Will the antihistamine be metabolized by tomorrow morning so that it won't be passed on to my baby in the breast milk?*

2. *I won't be able to finish this sandwich today. How can I keep it from "going bad" before tomorrow?*

3. *When my daughter mixes baking soda and vinegar for her science project, she sees fuming and foaming and calls it a volcano. Why is it that nothing happens when I mix oil and vinegar, but she gets that cool reaction when she mixes baking soda and vinegar?*

4. *Hot packs and cold packs don't look all that different, but they surely behave differently once you hit or squeeze them. Why does one get hot and one get cold?*

FIGURE 6.10

DISCUSSION QUESTIONS IN FRESHMAN CHEMISTRY

Exploring Connections of Frameworks to Real-World Problems

Notes

1. This question as well as some of the others in this chapter were written by my colleague George Gurria, who generously shared materials and ideas with me when I first started teaching at Alverno.

2. This assessment was created by my colleague, Kay Davis, who has helped me tremendously to understand how to think developmentally in designing course experiences and assessments.

3. *Ability-Based Learning Program: The Chemistry Major* (Milwaukee: Alverno College Institute, 2002).

4. *Modeling the Unseen,* from *The World of Chemistry* (Santa Barbara: The Annenberg/CPB Collection, 1989).

5. See, for example, the *Prentice-Hall Molecular Model Set for Organic Chemistry* (Englewood Cliffs, New Jersey: Prentice Hall, 1984).

6. Beau Fly Jones, Jean Pierce, and Barbara Hunter, "Teaching Students to Construct Graphic Representations," *Educational Leadership* (December 1988/January 1989), 20–25.

PART FOUR

THE STUDENT PERSPECTIVE

In the opening paragraph of her chapter, Rebecca Valentine writes that "using the disciplines I've learned is second nature; it's become as much a part of who I am as what I do." She proceeds to reflect on the kind of learning she experienced during her college education and how she has continued not only to apply, but also to transform, that learning in different dimensions of her life, truly using disciplines as frameworks for lifelong learning. She would be the first to say that her experience should not be construed as representative of all students at Alverno College, but there are dimensions of it that certainly resonate with much of what the other authors say in their chapters and that characterize what would be a common experience for many students. This is especially significant since she did not even see the chapter on her major, English, before she wrote hers.

7

BECAUSE HESTER PRYNNE WAS AN EXISTENTIALIST, OR WHY USING THE DISCIPLINES AS FRAMEWORKS FOR LEARNING CLARIFIES LIFE

Rebecca Valentine

When I first sat down to write this chapter, I reluctantly admitted to an underlying but pervasive concern: How can I write an entire chapter on the topic of using disciplines as frameworks for learning? Is there that much to say? Obviously there is, because you're reading an entire book on the subject. And as I read through papers and various assignments I had written while a student at Alverno College, I was delighted to be able to track my development as a learner. I realized then why I was hesitating to get started writing this chapter—not that I had nothing to say, but that the approach to learning I developed at Alverno has become such an integral facet of my everyday life that, in my mind, there is nothing unusual about it. For me, using the disciplines I've learned is second nature; it's become as much a part of who I am as what I do. So the trick is not in knowing what to say, but in figuring out how best to say it so that you understand how far-reaching this style of learning can be.

I came to Alverno in my mid-twenties after having made my living as a singer in a rock band, an administrative assistant to several high-level executives, and a human resources liaison for a predominantly white, upper-class school district. I had a high school record that reflected terrific grades, but that revealed none of the desperate boredom that accompanied me throughout those four years. By senior year, I had stopped thinking for myself in the classroom because anything I had to say seemed only to distract the teacher and deter progress. Although I knew I'd eventually attend college, I decided to experience life unencumbered by homework for a while, so I put off higher education until I could muster the enthusiasm I would need to make the journey worthwhile. When I entered Alverno, it was with the goal of getting a B.A. in English; I had no idea the degree would turn out to be merely the bonus. Alverno's faculty and their dedication to student-centered learning showed me a world I didn't know existed. The me who started college in 1991 was but a shadow of the me who graduated in 1995.

How You Learn and Why It Matters

Using disciplines as frameworks for learning allows us to exist in an almost limitless state because it encourages us to learn using the methods we find most effective. For example, I majored in English. Why? Because I had a lifelong affinity for reading and learning through applied texts. I minored in philosophy. Why? Because I am a person who likes to analyze issues from multiple perspectives. I like to argue; I like to imagine the what-ifs and see where the free association realm takes me. I also minored in professional communication. Why? Because I've always been a realist, and I knew it would serve me well to develop my sense of business as well as my technology skills.

For all these reasons, I didn't major in science or nursing or social science. I believe we're born with an open capacity for learning what we instinctively enjoy and appreciate, and each field requires its own exact abilities, though often they overlap. By using disciplines as frameworks for learning, students are encouraged to nurture the abilities they already naturally (even if subconsciously) value and apply them to studies in areas that might otherwise intimidate them. Learning, then, becomes a habit.

How Albert Camus Helped Me Understand
Nathaniel Hawthorne

Arguably the most significant moment in my learning actually involved making connections across disciplines. I can still clearly remember the day I realized that Hester Prynne was an existentialist, although this moment happened more than a decade ago.

Hester is the protagonist of Nathaniel Hawthorne's romance, *The Scarlet Letter.* Hester lives in colonial New England, when Puritanism is all the rage. A young, robust woman married to an older, crotchety man, Hester forsakes her marriage vows and falls in love with a young minister who lives in town. They consummate their forbidden love, and the result is a daughter, Pearl. The townspeople discover Hester's adultery, and they force her to wear a giant red "A" on her bodice to serve as both a private and public reminder of her sin. She is exiled to a life of loneliness with only her beloved Pearl for companionship.

This was my second reading of *The Scarlet Letter,* and because I had the luxury of already knowing the plot and the outcome, I found myself focusing more on the themes of the novel as well as the underlying philosophy. Days after reading this novel in a literature class, I began studying two texts in philosophy: "The Myth of Sisyphus" and "An Absurd Reasoning," both by Albert Camus. These texts deal with the philosophy of absurd reasoning, which, in a nutshell, states that once we realize that life is meaningless, to choose to continue living is an act of revolt. Camus's essay, "An Absurd Reasoning," explains his philosophy, while "The Myth of Sisyphus" illustrates it in the parable of the man pushing the rock up the mountain, knowing all the while that it will only roll back down and that he will have to repeat his efforts.

I read the Camus texts several times, each time "getting it" a little more. And I found myself thinking about values, and the meaning—or lack of it—in life, and the relationship between freedom and responsibility. The major framework, at least as I interpret it, of philosophy is that philosophical theory can be applied to practically everything. So though my major was English, a great deal of my processing was more closely related to philosophy, both in and out of class.

During this time frame, I entered my Early American Literature course prepared to discuss Hawthorne's novel, and as I was putting in my two cents about why Hester Prynne made the choices she did, the proverbial lightbulb lit up. "She was an existentialist!" I excitedly proclaimed. I gave a brief explanation of what we were studying in my philosophy course and described how Hester's choices and behavior exhibited an underlying absurd reasoning.

Hester could have chosen death by announcing that the minister with whom she committed adultery was still alive and living in the townspeople's midst. Both parents and child would have been put to death. Instead, she chose to live her life of exile with a positive attitude. She led a modest life, assisted with local charities, and expected nothing from anyone. At one point in the novel, Hawthorne emphasizes his protagonist's awareness of the futility of her existence. She knows she'll always be an outcast, a woman scorned. At the same time, she recognizes the scarlet letter, which she has intricately adorned with embroidery of golden thread, as her salvation in that no one demands from her what they demand from her peers. She is not expected to be a productive citizen, or pious, or even ladylike. She isn't expected to *be* anything at all. And so it is in her punishment that she finds freedom.

This made me think of Camus's "Sisyphus," in which he says, "The lucidity that was to constitute his torture at the same time crowns his victory. There is no fate that cannot be surmounted by scorn." Hester, by being conscious of her situation (a life of torment), conquered it and led a fulfilling life, one of passion, freedom, and, finally, revolt. She embraced the absurd—a life of deeper devotion and goodness than that exhibited by most unstigmatized people, and one that would go unrewarded—and won. Her attitude of scorn toward her punishment was her triumph, her revolution.

Aside from the excitement I felt at being able to better understand a novel I already appreciated, and using that novel to more fully comprehend what I considered to be a confounding philosophy, I was fully aware that I had the great fortune to experience what my teachers had been talking about: the theory of cross-discipline learning. *This* is why they were all so enthusiastic about it! It's great to be able to see what you were doing in any given situation in hindsight; it's absolutely inspiring and incredible to be aware of the greatness of a moment as it is happening. I have experienced that feeling at other times in my life, four times as I was giving birth and once as I held the body of my dead child in the palm of my hand. The magnitude of the moment, the awareness that life will forever be changed, is an experience that stays with you and influences each moment that follows, great and small. When learning can be this powerful, why settle for less?

Part of the feedback from one of my philosophy professors assured me of what I had discovered. Her response to my cross-discipline learning experience was the following:

Doing what you do here is more than okay. It's realizing that much of the distinctions that exist between disciplines are false and that there is so much we can do with philosophical theory. By engaging *The Scarlet Letter* as a context through which to imagine Camus' meaning you demonstrate an ability to integrate ideas and relate them in a variety of contexts. I think Hester Prynne wonderfully exemplifies the meaning you are attempting to convey and this shows a close reading of the text . . .

Literary Frameworks: Not Just for Classroom Learning

In my studies as an English major at Alverno, I was introduced to eight frameworks of literary criticism:

- Mimetic (art reflects life), which includes two sub-frameworks, historic and Marxist
- New historicism (best understands literature within its historical context)
- Feminist (assumes there is a woman's way of knowing)
- Reader-response (reader creates meaning vs. finds meaning)
- Deconstructionist (meaning is not fixed because language is fluid)
- Psychoanalytic (involves critique of author; assumes writing and reading are inseparable from psychoanalysis)
- Biographical, also known as expressive (text is direct reflection of author, so to know one gives insight into the other)
- Formalist (meaning is inherent in the elements)

These frameworks became the basis for all of our studies, and we were required to know the elements that composed each one and demonstrate our knowledge in various assignments. You do this often enough, and it becomes second nature. Developing a mastery of these frameworks influenced my studies across the board; knowing which ones I favored gave me insight into how I was naturally inclined to read a text. It also gave me an edge in knowing which frameworks were most useful in analyzing particular texts. For example, in reading philosophy texts, I found application of the formalist framework most effective. How was the philosophy presented in terms of organizational elements? What the author chose to tell me and in what order, and how the points were illustrated, could often lend an understanding I might otherwise have had difficulty developing. The reader-response framework also greatly influenced my philosophical reading. This particular framework allowed for fluid, rather than static, meaning, and focused on the language used to convey meaning and message.

One particular example of using a literary framework to foster understanding in another discipline took place in a course on the civilizations and cultures of Latin America. One of the texts used to teach that course was Isabel Allende's *The House of Spirits*. The novel spans generations of one particular powerful family and its rise and subsequent fall from power. Reading the book was a truly eye-opening experience. I analyzed it using a particular reader response framework, that of "literature as socialization or protest." In doing so, I was struck by how much the novel could teach me about Latin American culture. By considering Allende's novel one of protest, my own perspective of patriarchy, feminism, conservatism, and radicalism were enhanced. My worldview grew a thousandfold as I read the account of the lives of these fictional—yet representational—characters. By choosing the literature as protest framework, I got a greater feel for and understanding of not only Latin America's history, but of the different effects that history has had on people in terms of class, gender, political views, and so forth. What's more, I was open to learning about the culture itself and the importance of the role of spirituality, the supernatural, and the resiliency of Latin American women.

I could have chosen any one of the numerous models for learning for my formal analysis of Allende's novel, and, without doubt, I subconsciously applied several during my reading. For me, English isn't really something you learn, but more of a *method* of learning. You don't learn English; you use the models and frameworks of the discipline to learn whatever it is you seek. Whatever else you discover along your journey is a bonus. Had I used the feminist framework and its questions to analyze *The House of Spirits,* I might have come away from my reading with a response different from the one I had using the literature as protest model. Or I could have used the new historicism approach, with yet a different result. Depending on what model(s) you use in your analysis, you'll finish with different details that eventually lead you to the same place, to that complete picture the writer was trying to create. I found power in mastering those literary models because they allowed me to investigate texts in ways I might not have considered on my own.

Application beyond the Classroom: Lifelong Learning

These basic frameworks became my strongest learning tools, and once I left Alverno, I came to the gradual, if not startling, realization that virtually every experience I had outside the classroom was informed by my command of these tools. For the sake of clarity, I'll divide the most profound experiences into two categories: personal and professional.

Personal

Although my mission in writing this chapter is to add a learner's perspective to the idea of using disciplines as frameworks for learning, it would be unfair to limit discussion to the classroom because, once you learn in that way, it has a domino effect. For example, I see my learning manifest itself very strongly in the way I parent. I was educated to use learning models for guidance rather than as rigid rules; I was encouraged to facilitate my own learning and then work with the outcomes.

Although I am by nature a reflective person, that tendency was indirectly nurtured and enhanced by my Alverno experience because much of our focus was on learning how to accurately self assess. Our goal was not only to do well enough to satisfy the criteria, but to be able to figure out *on our own* where we did well, where there was room for improvement, and, ultimately, why we either succeeded or failed. After four years of self assessing on a regular basis, I recognized that doing so had become a habit of mind; I do it without consciously realizing it. And this ability largely informs the way in which I parent my four children.

I make a conscious choice to mother my kids with consideration for feelings and experiences as well as a recognition of individual temperaments and emotional intelligences, something my own teachers modeled for me. I don't always succeed; I admit to having said, "Because I said so," now and then. But those instances are few and far between, and that's why I've been exhausted for eleven years. I'd move mountains to do right by my kids, though, and I know my job is to help them unlock their potential in every possible way while still being able to function in the real world. In order to help them do that, I make the daily effort to teach them how to self assess.

When my five-year-old daughter approaches me with a drawing she's created and the question, "Do you think this is good?" I don't automatically say, "Yes." I tell her what I like about it, and then I ask her if *she* thinks it's good. Usually she does, but always she points out something she'd like to make better—a tree, an animal, a person's face. And then she goes about making her improvements. My eleven-year-old son, Max, has also developed the ability to self assess, as demonstrated when he brings me a paper he's written for school. He'll hand it to me with a comment such as, "I need to develop this paragraph more," or "I don't like the way I've described that character, but I'll fix it." Sometimes he'll say something like, "I think I did a good job with this scene." And always, he wants only my opinion before he hands in the assignment; he doesn't ask me how to improve upon it, or to check his work. In fact, I can't recall ever being asked by any of my kids, "How am I doing?" In his or her own way, each of them is already beginning to establish a standard on which personal progress is based. I wish I'd had that sense of empowerment as a child, rather than having been taught to see what grade the teacher gave me (or what compliment an adult bestowed upon me) before determining how well or poorly I performed.

I write a weekly newspaper column entitled "The Family Room." Judging by the reactions of my readers and the happiness of my editor, the column is successful. I write about what I know: family life. The tone of my column is a cross between Erma Bombeck and Anna Quindlen, and it covers all aspects of raising kids. I write about the ugly stuff—divorce, losing your temper, death—as readily as I do the lighter moments. I am no authority on the topics of which I write; I am merely a voice, one that readers can relate to and appreciate.

What these readers may not know—but what I am sure of—is that I am using my ability to reflect on those fleeting moments that make life worth living. I do not write of anything extraordinary; it is a column about ordinary circumstances. Each week I share something from my own experience and apply it to a more universal musing. If not for my ability to self assess, to ask myself the tough questions and apply my findings to the larger picture with brutal honesty, it is a column that would go unwritten. As it is, I am able to touch the lives of people in small—but not insignificant—ways.

Philosophizing has also played an important role in my job as a mom. As it was in my English studies, so it was in my philosophy classes. It was my responsibility to ask questions—the right questions—to reach an understanding or comprehension of an abstract concept. Asking questions, when stripped to its most radical element, is nothing more than self-directed learning. I do that all the time when parenting my kids. I encourage them to ask questions before making choices or forming opinions. I want them to question authority (not mine, of course) rather than to blindly accept what is, simply because it is what has always been.

Professional

I make my living as a writer and editor in a home office. My client base is diverse, and not one of the companies has the same, or even similar, needs as the other. I provide writing and/or editing services for an accounting firm that specializes in clergy taxes, a Christian curriculum/nonfiction book publisher, a Web-based retailer, a reference book publishing company, an office supply store, a taxonomist, and the list goes on. The only commonality among my clients is that they need someone who can put into words what they want to say. And it's probably safe to say that anyone who makes a living by writing could satisfactorily complete the task. I like to think I give my clients something they can't get elsewhere, though. And when all the niceties are stripped away, what remains is this: I commit to my clients on a level made possible only by careful consideration of their perspective.

This consideration goes beyond asking basic questions and involves a certain amount of intuition, of knowing how to approach a topic or issue so that the final result is a text that is accurately representative of each individual client. In other words, I can't write something that sounds like me. In order to step outside my own skin, I have to be able to imagine that I am writing about my own business or product. This can be especially difficult when I can't relate to a specific project. But these more challenging projects are also the ones I enjoy the most, because they require more from me not so much as a writer or editor, but as a thinker.

Because of the diversity of my clients' businesses, it is inevitable that I won't always agree wholeheartedly with the texts I edit. Yet still I must do my utmost to give each client a legible, aesthetically pleasing book manuscript. In order to do this, I separate my personal self from my professional self, and I edit with an eye attuned to the finer details. In other words, I deconstruct the text and take into consideration one aspect at a time. Deconstruction is one of the critical frameworks I learned in my English studies. I remember my first reaction to this framework: I hated it. It seemed cold, detached from the text and the way I had always valued literature, which was for its meaning and comprehensiveness. Deconstruction assumes that language refers only to itself rather than to an extratextual reality, so I had little use for it and avoided it whenever possible. So you can imagine my delight when I discovered a use for it in my professional life.

When I work on an editing project for a client, I may find myself reading content that sometimes leads me to feel resentment or anger or disbelief. In order to suspend those feelings, I remind myself that deconstruction is a criticism that claims that any meaning of text is mere accident in relation to my intentions. When doing that, I am able to read without bias. I can fix errors in such a way that the author's meaning is not changed, even if I'd like it to be. I also employ, once again, the reader-response framework when reading and editing these texts. I consider my own experience with what the text is saying and use that as a basis for my editorial decisions.

In addition to running my own business, I teach adult extension courses at one of our state universities. I teach writing and business courses that run four hours a week for four weeks. Writing and editing are solitary endeavors, and I value the social interaction that comes with teaching. My student feedback sheets often comment on my ability to make the subject understandable. My students think I'm fun. Remember, these are adults who have spent at least an eight-hour day on the job. They've grabbed a quick bite to eat on the way to the campus, and then they expect to sit and listen to me.

But that's the trick. They don't just sit and listen. I pull the chairs into a circle for the beginning of class. We talk about things that have nothing to do with the subject at hand for about ten or fifteen minutes, and then we get down to business. I don't burden them with lots of handouts or overheads; I talk, they talk back. I have at my desk a very brief outline of what I need to address. But I don't lecture all the time. Instead, I ask very specific questions whose answers tell me what kind of learners my students are. Then, when it comes to small group work, I break them down into groups according to how they seem to learn best, and we take it from there. I have found that this method works well in my particular setting. And while this partitioning might seem like a no-brainer, it isn't. A quick look into the classrooms as I make trips down the hallways tells me that most of the extension classes are being taught the old-fashioned way, with forward-facing tables in rows, the teacher in front, the students taking notes. When I see this, I can't help but wonder if those students are getting their money's worth.

Aside from developing discipline-related frameworks and learning models, every student at Alverno relearns how to learn. I remember the surprise

I experienced in my first semester of a basic social science course when the instructor had us do group work. Group work required that everyone participate and contribute. There was going to be no getting by on the efforts of others. I quickly found out how effective this method of learning is, and I readily adapted to it. So when I was hired to teach, it only made sense to replicate that atmosphere.

I believe my attitude toward teaching adults helps me design learning in a way students find useful. Some of my students are homemakers; others are engineers. Some are college students, and still others are corporate executives. While I can find some level on which to relate to each and every one of them, I can in no way know what their daily lives are like. And so I teach with the attitude that I have as much to learn from them as they do from me. Again, this teacher–learner reciprocity comes from my experience at Alverno. We didn't call instructors "Professor this or that," but instead used their first names. Their office doors weren't closed when we passed by; we could drop in unannounced, or accost them in the cafeteria. Just as it is in disciplines, the distinction between teacher and student was only faintly drawn, and never static. I know when I'm teaching a class that I'm teaching it only because it happens to concern a topic of which I am knowledgeable. The tables could easily be turned, and I could be a student of one of my students if the subject were different. I actually find that each student brings something of value in his or her particular experiences, and because we operate in an interactive learning environment, the student is able to share that valuable insight.

I consider the method of learning worth discussing in this chapter because it really is inseparable from everything else I talk about here. Using disciplines as frameworks for learning seems to be an evolutionary concept, but its success depends upon having an atmosphere open to individuality, emotion, and the possibility—if not the expectation—of the volatility often involved in the development and exchange of ideas. I once was verbally attacked by another student in an ethics class because I suggested that nonhuman life has intrinsic value completely separate from the value we humans attribute to it and that, as a whole, society does not recognize that value. My peer completely lost her temper and began shouting at me in the middle of my presentation. Rather than taking offense, I was thrilled that something I had to say stirred up enough emotion to truly rattle another's cage. Strangely enough, this classmate gave me terrific feedback, indicating that I had made her consider an idea she had not previously entertained. She also privately apologized to me. I doubt the subjects I teach will ever cause outbursts of this degree, but it's encouraging to know that in the proper setting, learning doesn't become something you do, but rather a particular approach to life.

When All Is Said and Done

I have always had an inquiring mind; it has been both a blessing and a curse. My learning experience at Alverno fostered my ability to see complexity— even ambiguity—in the world around me not as something to surmount or overcome, but as integral to the mystery of life and people in general. My tendency to investigate and reflect, to get lost in free association thinking, was encouraged in my study of English and philosophy. The more I learned, the more I realized I didn't need to actually study my disciplines. Rather, I needed to allow them to happen to me and then process the experience.

In an external assessment, which involved a formal presentation students made to their faculty in order to prove the appropriate level of mastery in our major, I was required to demonstrate the ability "to identify and use literary frameworks knowledgeably as tools of interpretation." I received extensive feedback on all my performances, but the following is most relevant to the idea of disciplines as frameworks for learning: "This is a real strength for you . . . You were able to relate Dukes' novel not only to literary frameworks . . . but to broader disciplinary frameworks as well, showing us how *Saving St. Germ* is about social science, history, philosophy, and so on. It was clear to all of us that frameworks are a natural part of your thinking now." Ten years later, that feedback still holds true. Poet Audre Lorde said, "The learning process is something you can incite, literally incite, like a riot." What a gift it would be to our society if all educators understood that they hold such power.

INDEX